A Guide to The New Church's Teaching Series

The New
Church's Teaching Series

A Guide to
The New
Church's
Teaching Series

Linda L. Grenz

COWLEY PUBLICATIONS
Cambridge · Boston
Massachusetts

The title *The Church's Teaching Series* is used by permission of the Domestic and Foreign Missionary Society. Use of the series title does not constitute the Society's endorsement of the content of the work.

Library of Congress Cataloging-in-Publication Data:
Grenz, Linda L., 1950–
    A guide to using the New church's teaching series / Linda Grenz.
    p. cm. — (The new church's teaching series ; v. 13)
    Includes bibliographical references.
    ISBN 1-56101-180-0 (alk. paper)
    1. New church's teaching series. 2. Christian education—Textbooks—Anglican. 3. Episcopal Church—Doctrines—Study and teaching. I. Title. II. Series.
BX5874 .G74 2000
268'.8373—dc21   00-031435

Cynthia Shattuck and Vicki Black, editors
Cover design by Vicki Black. Cover art: *Polyphonic White* (1930) by Paul Klee.

This book was printed by Transcontinental Printing in Canada on recycled, acid-free paper.

Cowley Publications
28 Temple Place • Boston, Massachusetts 02111
800-225-1534 • www.cowley.org

Table of Contents

Chapter One

Using The New Church's Teaching Series

The New Church's Teaching Series, like its predeces-
sors, is primarily designed for adult Christian formation. While many people may simply want to read
the books on their own, the series will be far more
useful in a congregational context if you use them as
the basis for your adult education program.

The original Church's Teaching Series, launched in
1949, was designed to give its readers a sense of
Anglican identity—who we are as Anglicans and what
makes us similar to and different from other
Christians. It was developed under the auspices of the
national church and was offered as the Episcopal
Church's "official teaching." As the editor of the current series, James E. Griffiss, explains in his preface to
each volume, this series differs in two significant
ways: "It has no official status, claims no special
authority, speaks in a personal voice, and comes not
out of committees but from scholars and pastors
meeting and talking informally together." This series
is also designed for a different readership: "adults who

are not 'cradle Anglicans,' but who come from other religious traditions or from no tradition at all, and who want to know what Anglicanism has to offer."

This series, therefore, is uniquely designed to speak to the church as we find ourselves today. It addresses more topics than the earlier series and it covers each topic both at a more introductory level and with a broader perspective. This responds to the likelihood that the readers will be less familiar with the Episcopal Church and the Anglican Communion than before; at the same time, the increasing globalization of our society demands a broader perspective on the world, its complexity, and the range of issues facing members of the church.

One of the key factors facing the Episcopal Church today is that a large proportion of adult members are not "formed" by the theology, doctrine, or traditions of the Episcopal Church. The adults that make up the baby boom generation present an interesting challenge to congregations. They are seekers—old enough and experienced enough to know that their lives are missing something and they want to find whatever that something is. However, they have largely been absent from the church since their early teen years, so their knowledge and understanding of the faith and life of the Episcopal Church (which changed significantly in their absence) is minimal. On top of that, this is the most highly educated cohort group in recorded human history. Consequently, their expectations of themselves and the church are high. They do not like to admit that they do not know something, so they want to gain information quickly and in ways that fit into already over-booked lives.

The New Church's Teaching Series is ideally suited for this population. Each book has six to eight chapters—about the number of sessions today's adults are likely to commit to attending at one time. When taken as a whole, the volumes in the series actually provide a complete four-year adult education program; however, since most adults today find such a long commitment difficult to make, each volume can stand on its own.

Most churches will increase class attendance by starting with groups short in duration and time. In other words, you can offer a weekly 45-minute session on one book that lasts no more than about eight weeks and then start a new course. You may find you will gradually need to extend the time the group spends on each chapter. You can do this by negotiating with the group to come earlier or stay later so your Sunday morning group is at least an hour or even longer. Or, you can move the sessions to afternoons or evenings and have a 2-hour session. If you use good small group process, the group will bond and mature and naturally seek more time together and more depth. (See the suggested 45-minute session and 2-hour session plans in chapter four.)

Even if you move to longer meeting times or evening sessions, it is still best to have a Sunday morning option that is short in duration and time. These short groups allow newcomers and others to join at any time and to make a minimal investment of time and energy. They serve as "entry ports" for those who might otherwise never risk joining an ongoing group.

One final suggestion: invite members of the vestry or mission committee to lead these discussions in teams. This method was used by Emmanuel Memorial Church in Champaign, Illinois. They did about one book per "semester," sometimes selecting a book that related to a current "hot topic" in the diocese, church, or world. They discovered that attendance was high and people valued seeing their vestry members in a spiritual leadership role rather than functioning only as management. It also broadened the perspective of the vestry members and developed their leadership skills.

∿ The Books in the Series

Included in this section is a brief description of each book and its author along with a list of the chapters so you can see what is covered and how many "sessions" each book contains. The books are cross-referenced in a chart at the end of chapter two with groups that might find them particularly helpful; each group is also discussed in more detail in that chapter.

Volume 1: The Anglican Vision

Summary

This volume provides an introduction to the Anglican tradition, including the origins of Anglicanism, the catholic and evangelical renewal movements of the nineteenth century, and a survey of Anglican mission, theology, and worship. The author focuses especially on Anglicanism's ability to hold together theological continuity with social and cultural change because of its particular grasp of the meaning of the Incarnation—the Good News of God dwelling in and among us.

Author

James E. Griffiss is the editor of the *Anglican Theological Review* and the series editor of The New Church's Teaching Series. An Episcopal priest and theologian, he has taught systematic theology at several Episcopal seminaries in North America and was recently named Canon Theologian for the Episcopal Church by Presiding Bishop Frank Griswold. He is the author and editor of a number of books, including *To Believe is to Pray: Readings from Michael Ramsey.*

Chapters (8)
Part I: The Origins of Anglicanism
1. From England to Portage
2. The Beginnings of Anglicanism
3. The Renewal of Anglicanism
4. Mission and the Anglican Communion
Part II: Anglican Belief and Practice
5. Anglican Believing
6. Anglican Worship
7. Identity and Diversity
8. The Church as Sacrament

Volume 2: Opening the Bible

Summary
This book helps us navigate the practical difficulties of reading the Bible, explaining why the pages look the way they do, how to compare translations, and how to use notes and cross-references. More importantly, the author teaches us the importance of respectfully approaching the Bible as scripture: it is a book with a long history, complex traditions, and diverse author-ship, and it must be read on its own terms. This book offers ways of reading the Bible today that are grounded in the ways Anglicans have read scripture from the time of Tyndale and Cranmer.

Author
Roger Ferlo is the rector of the Church of St. Luke in the Fields in New York City, and has led studies of the Bible in a number of parishes and dioceses. Before his ordination as an Episcopal priest, he earned a Ph.D. in literature and taught English at Yale University.

Chapters (6)
1. Why Read the Bible?
2. Preparing to Read
3. Scanning the Page
4. Comparing Translations
5. Interpreting the Explanatory Notes
6. Reading the Bible, Reading Scripture

Volume 3: Engaging the Word
Summary
This volume teaches us how to use critical and practical tools to explore the Hebrew and Christian scriptures intelligently and perceptively by asking, What did they mean for their original audience? What do they mean for us today? The author introduces us to the key terms and concepts used by biblical scholars to understand the literal, historical, and prophetic meanings of the Bible. He explores scripture passages that touch on ethical questions, the nature of God, the teaching of Jesus, and themes of liberation and eschatology.

Author
Michael Johnston is the rector of Grace Church in Oak Park, Illinois, and has taught Bible studies in a number of parish groups. He has also taught homiletics at Seabury-Western Theological Seminary and in the Diocesan School for Deacons, and has studied and traveled extensively in the Holy Land.

Chapters (8)
1. Telling the Story
2. Passing on the Story
3. Making the Story Our Own
4. Breaking Open the Word
5. Forming Community Character

6. Who is the God of the Bible?
7. Who is the Jesus of the Bible?
8. The Word as Sacrament

Volume 4: *The Practice of Prayer*

Summary

This down-to-earth book on the essentials of prayer answers many of the common questions of the spiritual life, such as: How do we learn to listen to God in our prayer? How do we develop a life of prayer in the midst of busy, active lives? The author includes practical descriptions of the ways Christians have prayed through the centuries, from using the Jesus Prayer or rosary to praying with the stories of scripture and prayer book liturgies. She also discusses basic matters of Christian practice, including making a confession, intercession, going on retreat, simplifying our lives, using a journal to pray, finding a spiritual director, and praying through times of desolation.

Author

Margaret Guenther is an Episcopal priest, spiritual director, and retreat leader. She recently retired as professor of ascetical theology at The General Theological Seminary in New York City, where she was the director of its Center for Christian Living. Her other books include *Holy Listening: The Art of Spiritual Direction* and *Toward Holy Ground: Spiritual Directions for the Second Half of Life.*

Chapters (10)
Part I: Spirituality and Prayer
1. An Introduction to Spirituality
2. Prayer as Conversation
3. Varieties of Prayer
4. Prayer Through the Centuries

5. Practices of Prayer
Part II: Praying in the Midst of Life
6. Finding God in the Ordinary
7. Prayer and Parenting
8. Learning Simplicity
9. Praying Through Desolation
10. Praying in Community

Volume 5: Living With History

Summary
This book introduces us to how history shapes the church as we know it. Rather than offering a chronological list of events, Fredrica Harris Thompsett focuses on the living traditions and memories that inform the church's identity and mission today. She begins by discussing the relationship between history, tradition, and change, and goes on to look at three of the ways that Anglicans have handled conflict and controversy throughout history. She then discusses how theological and historical insight can be "recycled" to shed new light on the problems of today.

Author
Fredrica Harris Thompsett is professor of church history at the Episcopal Divinity School in Cambridge, Massachusetts. A popular conference leader, lecturer, and participant in world-wide Anglican dialogue, she is also the author of *We are Theologians* and *Courageous Incarnation.*

Chapters (6)
1. Living with History
2. Ten Touchstones of History
3. The Ministry We Share
4. Living with Controversy
5. Recycling Tradition

6. New Occasions Teach New Duties

Volume 6: *Early Christian Traditions*
Summary

This volume introduces us to the world of the early church and faith. Beginning with the Jewish, Greek, and Roman cultures in which the first followers of Jesus lived and worshiped, Rebecca Lyman explores the development of the church's theology, worship, leadership, and moral life during the first six centuries. How did a small group of believers on the margins of Judaism emerge as the established religion of the Roman Empire? It is this story of intense religious fervor, theological controversy, and persecution that shaped the church of Christendom in the middle ages and established the apostolic tradition.

Author
Rebecca Lyman is an Episcopal priest and professor of church history at the Church Divinity School of the Pacific in Berkeley, California. A popular teacher and lecturer, she has also been a translator for *The New American Bible*. Her research and writing focus on the early history of the church and its definition of orthodoxy and heresy.

Chapters (8)
1. Anglican Identity and Christian Traditions
2. The World of the Early Church: *Romans, Jews, and Christians*
3. Apostolic Christianity: *The Gnostic Controversies*
4. Christianity and Social Crisis: *Persecution, Unity, and Holiness*
5. Imperial Christianity: *The Desert and the City*
6. Who is Jesus? *Early Images of Christ*

7. Who is God? *Credal Orthodoxy from Nicaea to Augustine*
8. The Church in Late Antiquity: *Saints and Sinners in the City of God*

Volume 7: Opening the Prayer Book

Summary
This book helps us understand why *The Book of Common Prayer* is such an important aspect of Anglican identity and life. Jeffrey Lee begins with the fundamental questions: What is common prayer? How does prayer book worship shape who we are as a church? He then turns to the development of liturgical patterns, from the time of Jesus through the Reformation to modern revisions of the prayer book. He examines in particular the liturgies of Holy Week and Easter, baptism, eucharist, and the daily office, with a view to understanding the way these services are rooted in the historical prayers of the church and at the same time reflect the living tradition of Christians today. Finally, Lee discusses the future of the prayer book within the Anglican Communion in light of demands for further revision and greater freedom to adapt the prayer book to local needs and beliefs.

Author
Jeffrey Lee is an Episcopal priest who has served parishes in Wisconsin and Indiana. A speaker, retreat conductor, and conference leader with a particular interest in liturgy, he is also active in the renewal of the diaconate, publishing articles and serving on the board of the North American Association for the Diaconate.

Chapters (8)
1. What is Common Prayer?
2. The Pattern of Prayer
3. The Prayer Book is Born
4. The American Prayer Book
5. A Baptismal Church
6. The Eucharist and Daily Office
7. Liturgy in Action
8. Looking Toward the Future

Volume 8: Mysteries of Faith

Summary
This volume on theology introduces the great mysteries of the Christian faith: the doctrines of creation,
revelation, incarnation, salvation, and eschatology,
which are all held together by the doctrine of the
Trinity. To explain these beliefs for Christians today,
particularly the Trinity, Mark McIntosh begins with
what we know: the language of relationship and
mutuality, of friendship and family ties. By drawing
on our common experiences as members of a community of faith, particularly through the sacraments of
baptism and eucharist, he helps us to explore these
mysteries for ourselves and to see how we might live
them in our daily lives.

Author
Mark McIntosh is an Episcopal priest in the Diocese of
Chicago and associate professor of systematic theolo-
gy and spirituality at Loyola University. He is the
author of _Christology from Within_ and _Mystical
Theology: The Integrity of Spirituality and Theology._

Chapters (7)
1. Mysteries of Faith
2. The New Encounter with God: _The Mystery_

of the Trinity
3. The Splendor of God: *The Mystery of Creation*
4. The Voice of God: *The Mystery of Revelation*
5. The Humanity of God: *The Mystery of the Incarnation*
6. The Glory of Humanity: *The Mystery of Salvation*
7. The Drama of the Cosmos: *The Mystery of Communion*

Volume 9: Ethics After Easter
Summary
This introduction to Christian moral thinking equips us with a distinctively Anglican approach to ethics, with its emphasis on holiness, sanctification, and the need for spiritual disciplines. Holmgren identifies clear axioms for Anglican moral theology and the methods required for moral decision-making on the part of individuals and church bodies. Other topics include the role of conscience and reason, the work of moral discernment, the difference between moral knowledge and saving knowledge, the meaning of natural law, and the value of consensus. The final chapter ends by giving readers a clear three-step methodology for building a moral case in Christian ethics, specifically on Christian involvement with war and acts of violence.

Author
Stephen Holmgren is associate professor of ethics and moral theology at Nashotah House, where he also works with two area medical ethics committees. He earned his doctorate at Oxford University, and is a popular conference leader and speaker. An Episcopal priest, he has served parishes in the dioceses of West Tennessee and Milwaukee.

Chapters (8)
1. The Walk From the Font
2. Seeking to Live a Good Life
3. The Book of Nature
4. The Book of Scripture
5. Laws, Manners, and Moral Principles
6. Sin, Character, and Conscience
7. Love in Acts, Rules, and Principles
8. Building a Case in Christian Ethics

Volume 10: Christian Social Witness

Summary
This volume on the social teachings of Anglicanism and the Episcopal Church presents a broad historical overview of Anglicanism's vision of a righteous social order, including the challenges of the new millennium. Beginning with the Bible's understandings of social justice, Lewis summarizes the Anglican witness of theologians like F. D. Maurice and William Temple and goes on to discuss the Episcopal Church in the nineteenth and early twentieth centuries. Later chapters discuss the challenges of a new social order that face the church today because of liberation theology, third-world debt and economic justice, and questions of race, gender, and human sexuality.

Author
Harold Lewis is the rector of Calvary Church in Pittsburgh, Pennsylvania, and the author of _Yet with a Steady Beat: The African American Struggle for Recognition in the Episcopal Church._ For many years he served the national church as staff officer for Black Ministries.

Chapters (8)
1. Social Justice and the Bible

2. The Anglican Social Witness
3. Social Justice in the Episcopal Church
4. Economic Justice
5. Racial Justice
6. Gender and Equality
7. Human Sexuality
8. Conclusion

Volume 11: Horizons of Mission
Summary
Arguing that Christian mission expresses God's longing to embrace all humanity in love, Titus Presler uses scripture, the history of mission, case studies, and the catechism to offer a fresh vision for mission in the multicultural environment of world Christianity. Most Episcopalians have had little exposure to how gospel understandings are being reshaped by Anglicans in Africa, Asia, and Latin America, Christianity's new center of gravity. Presler also explores how dioceses and parishes can engage fruitfully in world mission today.

Author
The son of missionary parents, Titus Presler grew up in India and later served as an Episcopal missionary with his family in Uganda. He holds a doctorate from Boston University in mission and the New Testament, and is now the rector of St. Peter's Church in Cambridge, Massachusetts.

Chapters (7)
1. The Dilemma of Mission Today
2. Mission Belongs to God
3. Learning from the History of Mission
4. The Anglican Mission Story
5. Gospel and Culture

6. An Anglican Vision for Mission
7. Engaging Your Parish in Mission

Volume 12: A Theology of Worship
Summary
In this book Louis Weil focuses on liturgy and worship in the Anglican tradition, exploring the nature of liturgical experience and prayer and offering a theology of liturgical prayer rather than an historical study. Weil believes the members of the faith community are the primary celebrants in the liturgy; in this light he considers the role of the ordained, multiculturalism, music, and the imperatives of including all members of the church—including children—in worship.

Author
An Episcopal priest and teacher of liturgy for almost four decades, Louis Weil is now professor of liturgics at the Church Divinity School of the Pacific. He has contributed to a number of ecumenical dialogues, and is the author of *Liturgy for Living, Sacraments and Liturgy: The Outward Signs, Gathered to Pray,* and over a hundred articles on liturgy.

Chapters (8)
1. Which Theology?
2. Who Celebrates?
3. Whose Culture?
4. Whose Idea of Beauty?
5. Whose Music?
6. Whose Sacraments?
7. Why Include Children?
8. Which Dance?

Volume 13: Christian Wholeness

Summary
This volume explores the journey to Christian wholeness and maturity as part of our "growing up" in Christ, a journey that begins in baptism and is nourished along the way by the sacraments of eucharist and reconciliation. By focusing on wholeness, Martin Smith suggests ways that we can gradually assume our new identity as Christians and come to recognize God's involvement in every aspect of our lives—including pain and suffering, love and desire, and the public world of economics, politics, and the arts. He sees human desire as the key to the spiritual life: desiring God enough to take risks and let down our defenses throughout a lifelong journey of conversion.

Author
Martin L. Smith, SSJE, is a member of the Society of St. John the Evangelist, a monastic order for men in the Episcopal Church with houses located in Cambridge and West Newbury, Massachusetts. An Episcopal priest, retreat leader, and spiritual director, he recently served as chaplain to the House of Bishops. His other books include *Reconciliation, Nativities and Passions, Love Set Free,* and *A Season for the Spirit.*

Chapters (6)
1. Christian Wholeness
2. Beginning with Baptism
3. Born Again and Growing Up
4. God's Way of Being Becomes Ours
5. Knowing Christ
6. Christ Wholly Present

Chapter Two

How to Use the Series

~ Audience and Meeting Format

Before you decide how to use the books in The New Church's Teaching Series it is important that you clearly identify who will be using them and in what way. Since the books are written for an adult audience, most programs will be for adults. However, you will still need to decide which adult groups. Do you plan to focus on younger adults or older adults? Singles or couples? Existing groups or new groups? Current members or newcomers? Will you fit the series into an existing educational program or are you developing a new one? Do you plan to gather people by interest, by occupation, by neighborhood, or according to their involvement in other church activities?

The answers to these questions will help you look at the second consideration: What format will you use? If you are fitting the series into an existing program, you might find it helpful to use a similar format or, conversely, it may add life to the program if you change it. The adult education forum, for example, is generally a presentation followed by discussion.

If this format works well, it might be helpful to continue it; if it is not working, you might try using a small group discussion format instead.

Before you decide on a format, look at the larger picture and identify the educational and developmental needs of your congregation. Then choose the time and format accordingly. You will need to decide whether to meet in one large group or several small groups. Will you meet on Sunday morning or in an afternoon/evening session? Will you include a meal and fellowship time or just study? Will you fit into existing committee or ministry meetings? Will you have a single leader, a leadership team, or rotating leadership? Will you incorporate related videos, guest speakers, and other activities, or just use the books? Will you use the study questions provided in the books, or will you generate your own?

～ Choosing the Books

There are many ways you can use some or all of the books in The New Church's Teaching Series, and here we will identify common groups in congregations and offer suggestions for which books might be most appropriate in those contexts. A table is provided at the end of this chapter that cross-references the books and church groups, giving you a quick overview of our suggested uses.

Once you are ready to begin selecting books to offer to the congregation as an adult education program, you will need to think about the order in which to use them. Obviously, you can simply use them in the order in which they were published, beginning with The Anglican Vision. Or you can solicit input from potential participants and start with the books that generate the most interest. Or you can simply start with what you and/or the planning group believe would appeal to the broadest group of people. Our guess is that most congregations will start with *The Anglican Vision, Opening the Prayer Book,* or *Opening the Bible.*

You will also want to think about timing. Will you pace the books in the series by season? If so, it makes sense to select a longer book (like *Opening the Prayer Book*) to start in September, when you have at least eight weeks to Advent, and a shorter one (like *Opening the Bible*) for an Advent study. Epiphany and Eastertide vary in length from year to year, so you will need to adjust accordingly. Lent might be a good time to focus on *The Practice of Prayer, Christian Wholeness,* or *Mysteries of Faith.*

Another timing question is: Will you hold the classes in successive weeks or take breaks in between them? It is best to avoid breaks of more than two weeks if you want small groups to bond and stay together. Sometimes a holiday or holy day will intervene—for example, do not bother scheduling a session on Christmas or Easter! The best "break" is to do the activity suggested for the book just completed or, where appropriate, for the next book (see chapter 5). Open those activity sessions to the entire congregation and move them to a larger room (like the fellowship hall) where the activity can attract the interest of others, who might then be moved to participate in the next book discussion.

Before selecting books to read, review what has happened in the congregation in the last couple of years. If you have had a series of adult education programs on a particular topic, it is probably best to put that topic later on the list—unless, of course, the book is a logical extension of what you have already done. Take time to look at your adult membership. Who normally attends and who does not attend adult education groups? Why or why not? What has been successful in the past and what has not worked? Why? Do you have many newcomers? What are the denominational backgrounds of your members? What are their levels of church experience? If necessary, do a short survey to make sure you know for whom you are planning this program.

Above all, ask people about their needs and interests—but be careful how you word the questions. If you ask them what they think you should offer, they will usually respond out of their "should's" and "ought's," rather than expressing what they want, need, or are likely to attend. Try asking, "What do you need that will help you be a more faithful disciple of Christ in the next year?" Or, "Which of the following topics would you attend six to eight sessions to learn more about?" Use a scale of 1 to 5: definitely=5, probably=4, maybe=3, unlikely=2, and no=1. Notice that the focus is on the likelihood of attending a group, not whether it is a good topic for the congregation. You want to know whether they will actually join a group to discuss this topic.

Another thing to consider is what your children and youth are doing in their educational program. Is there any special focus to their study that could be coordinated with the adult study? If, for example, the youth are learning about prayer, their parents might be interested in keeping up with them! Or, if the middle-school children are learning how to use the Bible, you might want to offer *Opening the Bible* or *Engaging the Word* to the adults.

Finally, consider the personal preferences and interests of the leaders. If the leader is excited about the topic, that will be communicated to the group. Go where there is energy! It is important to start with a book that at least sparks the interest of the leaders.

Tackle those books that seem less attractive to the leaders later in the program. Or, better yet, by then you might identify someone in the group who is interested in that topic and is willing to lead those sessions.

✧ Suggested Books for Education and Formation Programs

There are a variety of Christian formation programs in addition to general adult education, such as those for specific groups or ages. Formation programs may be ongoing or of short duration. The following suggestions are designed to assist you in incorporating The New Church's Teaching Series into these Christian formation programs.

Adult Education Forums

Most congregations have an adult education time, usually on Sunday mornings while the children and youth are attending their own education programs. Smaller congregations may have just one offering while larger congregations may have several different options. A popular format is the adult education forum, which often is a discussion of the sermon or some other topic introduced by the rector. Increasingly, the leadership for such classes is expanding to include lay people, who may lead the study of a book of the Bible, use videos, or lead the discussion of a series of books. Obviously, this is an ideal setting to introduce The New Church's Teaching Series, especially if the group is already accustomed to reading and discussing books together.

In congregations with multiple offerings there are several opportunities to introduce the books. You might, in fact, simply establish The New Church's Teaching Series as one option and address each book in turn. This would provide an ongoing group that people could come into at any time, and it would require minimal preparation time for the leaders, who would just need to read the week's chapter along with the rest of the group and prepare to lead the discussion using the questions provided.

Some congregations have afternoon or evening adult education opportunities. The most popular of these is the Lenten series. Again, the books of The New Church's Teaching Series can easily be used as the focus of such groups. *The Practice of Prayer, Engaging the Word, Opening the Prayer Book, Mysteries of Faith, Horizons of Mission, A Theology of Worship,* and *Christian Wholeness* might be especially appropriate. If you are establishing Lenten study groups, remember to make provision for childcare and consider including food, either a meal or dessert and coffee. Food encourages building relationships, which is a valuable part of the Christian formation process.

Young Adult Groups
Young adults, in particular, are likely to find the series books helpful. Many of them left the Episcopal Church as teenagers and have only recently returned, or they are coming from other denominations. Young adults tend to feel more comfortable meeting with their peers. You can help them find a place in the congregation by establishing a young adult group, which can be a separate group that meets during the regular adult education program times. It is better not to be too strict about specifying the age; usually just saying "the twenty-to-thirty–somethings group" is close enough. Let people decide for themselves if they fit in. Give the books to this group and encourage them to rotate the leadership—this age group is usually quite capable of leading themselves and usually enjoy a free-flowing collaboration. And again, food is good!

Young adults might start with *The Anglican Vision* if they are interested in what makes the Episcopal Church unique or with *The Practice of Prayer,* which responds to their likely interest in spirituality. *Opening the Bible, Engaging the Word, Opening the Prayer Book,* and *A Theology of Worship* can take them to the next level of worship life, while *Ethics After Easter* and *Christian Wholeness* are likely to address questions and concerns young adults bring to the church.

Bible Study Groups

Some congregations have an ongoing Bible study group that focuses on different books of the Bible. The group may meet on Sunday mornings or for a week-ly afternoon or evening session. It can be very helpful for this group to integrate learning about the Bible in general with their focus on specific books of the Bible. The obvious choices to start with are *Opening the Bible* and *Engaging the Word.* A logical next step for this group would be *The Practice of Prayer.* This group is also likely to be responsive to *Early Christian Traditions* and *Mysteries of Faith.*

People who are attracted to Bible study groups sometimes focus entirely on studying the scriptures. But study without action is deadening. This group may need to be encouraged to act on what they are hearing in the scriptures—to become engaged in some of the ministries being organized and planned by the outreach ministry group. So we recommend that this group also study *Christian Social Witness* and *Horizons of Mission*—even though they might not be their "nat-ural" choice for reading. They will, however, encour-age this group to study how the scriptures point to mission. You might even suggest that the Bible study and outreach ministry groups meet together as a way for them to enrich each other's perspectives and help the members of each group achieve more balance in their spiritual formation.

Foyer Meetings

Foyer meetings generally are informal in structure and usually include a meal in a parishioner's home. The host(s) invite a small group to a series of meetings. The focus of the group is usually fellowship, so much of the time is spent on getting to know one another. The afternoon or evening session concludes with some common discussion which, in this case, can focus on a chapter of the book being read and discussed. If you are using this model, it is easy simply to incorporate a book from the series, perhaps allowing people to sign up for a group based on their interest in the book scheduled for each host. Or, all of the groups might focus on the same book (for example, *The Anglican Vision* or *Christian Wholeness*) but gather in neighborhoods or around some other principle (age, occupation, and so on).

Small Group Ministry

Small groups have been shown to be very effective in building congregations, both spiritually and numerically. In an increasingly isolated world, small groups are a place where people can find community and be supported in their day-to-day struggles in living the faith. In recent years there has been substantial growth in small group ministries and many congregations already have established programs in place.

Discipleship Groups is a small group ministry program that was developed within the Episcopal Church.[1] It takes the church growth process and replaces the content (which often uses more evangelical language than many Episcopal congregations are accustomed to) with traditional Episcopal content—

the baptismal covenant and ministry in daily life. The content is not really what makes small groups work; rather, it is the process that is most important.

The methods suggested in Discipleship Groups can easily be adapted by congregations. Each group has a leader, an assistant leader, and an empty chair which is filled by a newcomer. When the group grows beyond twelve people it splits, with the assistant taking half of the group, and two new assistant leaders are identified and trained. This process provides a primary pastoral care unit as these groups support and minister to one another. They are also centers for Christian formation while serving as easy ways for new members to be integrated into the life of the congregation and grow in their knowledge and faith.

The books in The New Church's Teaching Series are ideal for small groups. If you want to develop a small group ministry with trained leadership and a structure like that described above, explore starting with Discipleship Groups or another small group ministry development program.

Newcomers

People who are new to a congregation often have much in common with other newcomers: they all have to learn what this congregation practices and believes. A newcomers group facilitates that learning and gives newcomers an opportunity to meet others who also are not part of the "in" group. Remember to build in ample social time—a meal or gathering in someone's home can help newcomers form relationships that make it easier to begin asking questions and discussing concerns in the group. It is also helpful to have the newcomers group led by the clergy and key leaders in the congregation because this gives newcomers a chance to identify with the congregation's leaders.

You might also invite a member of the vestry or other congregational leader to be part of the team and provide the primary leadership for the later sessions. Bonding with the clergy is important, but introducing laity early in this process helps newcomers avoid the trap of looking to the clergy for all that they need from the church.

The Anglican Vision is a logical book to start with in this group. *Opening the Prayer Book* and *Opening the Bible* are the other two books we would recommend for a series of four sessions (a social event plus three discussions) or eight sessions (a social event, two weeks per book, and a closing social event). *Early Christian Traditions*, *Christian Wholeness*, and *The Practice of Prayer* are three additional good choices for a newcomers' group.

Inquirers' Classes

A popular group in many congregations is the inquirers' class or its equivalent. The primary purpose of this group is to prepare adults for confirmation or reception and to give long-term members a refresher course on the church.

There are a couple of questions you need to address in planning for this group. First, how many sessions will you have? This may depend on your congregation's tradition ("We always have eight sessions just prior to the bishop's visit"), the preferences of the rector or other leaders, or the desires of the group. We encourage you to explore a variety of options for the length, including several evening sessions, a season (Lent would be especially appropriate), and a semester (fall or spring). You might also want to include an overnight retreat or an all-day session to enable the group to discuss topics in more depth.

The second question is: Who will lead it and what will be the format? Often the inquirers' class is led by the clergy. While it is certainly appropriate for clergy to be present, the leadership for this group can and should be shared with laity. If you have trained catechists leading the catechumenal process, they would be excellent candidates as leaders. Likewise, graduates of the Education for Ministry, or EFM, program can provide leadership for this group.[2] This is an opportunity for members of the vestry, lay readers, and other congregational leaders to participate in providing educational leadership.

If you are doing six to eight sessions (a common model), you will not be able to cover all the books in depth. So it is best to use one book per session as the topic for that session. The leader would read the book and do a presentation of about twenty minutes summarizing the important points in the book. Select about three or four questions to ask if you need them to get the discussion going—usually the participants will generate plenty of questions on their own. You can offer the books for those who wish to read them and, of course, point out that these books will be read and discussed in depth at various times during the coming years. This is a good way to introduce the topic and point participants to the next level of engagement.

A team of two or three people can lead the shorter version of this, especially once they are familiar with the books. If you have a longer timeframe, you might want to begin with the leaders doing the presentations and then ask the participants each to take responsibility for one of the books. One of the team leaders still needs to be prepared to step in in case the designated leader fails to show up or flounders. In some contexts this process will work very well; in others the group members may not be comfortable providing this kind of leadership. Select a method that is appropriate for your group.

If you are doing six to eight sessions we recommend:

1. *The Anglican Vision*
2. *Living With History* or *Early Christian Traditions*
3. *Opening the Prayer Book*
4. *Opening the Bible* or *Engaging the Word*
5. *The Practice of Prayer*
6. *Mysteries of Faith*
7. What is the commitment you make in confirmation/reception?

If you are doing a half-year (about twelve to fifteen sessions) we recommend:

1. *The Anglican Vision*
2. *Early Christian Traditions*
3. *Opening the Prayer Book*
4. *Opening the Bible*
5. *Engaging the Word*
6. *The Practice of Prayer*
7. *Mysteries of Faith*
8. *Ethics After Easter*
9. *Christian Wholeness*
10. *Christian Social Witness*
11. *Living With History*
12. *A Theology of Worship*
13. *Horizons of Mission*
14. What is the commitment you make in confirmation/reception?

If you are doing a full year (about twenty-six sessions) you can take the same list as above but spend two sessions with each of the books.

Catechumenal Process

The catechumenal process from the early church is being revived in the modern church. It is a process of formation for adults seeking to be baptized. The process is ongoing and catechumens (unbaptized adults) can join at any time. Each catechumen participates in specified liturgical events that lead up to baptism—ideally at the Easter Vigil.[3] Many clergy and congregations assume that most adults are already baptized, but this is not necessarily true. It is important to test that assumption by asking if people are baptized and to invite adults to consider baptism. You may be surprised by the number of adults in your congregation who are not baptized and who, given an opportunity, would consider baptism.

All of the books in The New Church's Teaching Series are valuable resources in this process. However, one cautionary note must be inserted here. The catechumenal process is *not* a program. It is inappropriate to assign the books to be read. The catechumenal process assumes that the catechists have read, studied, and know the information in these books and, as such, the series is ideal for the preparation of the catechists. But it is the role of the catechists to listen to the catechumens and to respond to where they are on their individual journeys. They might suggest a book to someone in the process, even one that the entire group might read and discuss. But this would be in response to the questions and needs of the catechumens, not according to some predetermined schedule. Often the books will serve as reference books for the catechists—a place to turn when the discussion leads to questions addressed by the books. So, for example, a catechist might pull one of the books off the shelf and find a section or a page to read aloud in response to a question or concern.

Other Established Adult Education Programs
There are a variety of established adult education programs in the church. If your congregation has or has had one of these programs, take some time to identify who attended those programs and how they might find the books of the series useful.

For example, one popular adult education program is Education for Ministry (EFM), a four-year program of theological education. This series fits with EFM in three ways. First, the series is a good "seed-bed" for future EFM participants. It lays the foundation for those who might then want to go even deeper. Second, the books can be used to supplement the materials provided in EFM. And third, graduates of EFM are likely candidates to help lead groups studying the series books. While not every EFM graduate has small group leadership skills, most of them have a depth of knowledge about the scriptures and theology that make them valuable members of a leadership team. *Kerygma* is another popular adult education program that might be the next step after reading the series books and again, its leaders and participants would be logical candidates for the leadership team.

Youth Programs
If your congregation uses a church school curriculum for youth, the teachers will find the series helpful in preparing specific lesson or series of lessons. For example, the *Episcopal Youth Curriculum* addresses a number of topics that correlate directly with the books.[4] For this and other comparable curricula, lead-

ers can read the corresponding book for background information and draw on the questions and activities suggested for that book to expand those lesson plans.

The popular *Journey to Adulthood* spiritual formation program includes curriculum within a complete youth program and offers numerous opportunities to use the series.[5] For example, there are about a dozen lesson plans on prayer to be spread over the first two years. *The Practice of Prayer* would be appropriate for the middle two years (J2A), either to read and discuss during lesson time or as evening reading material during the pilgrimage. The lesson on *The Book of Common Prayer,* which expects youth to develop an understanding of and lead the Sunday liturgy, would be greatly assisted by reading and discussing *Opening the Prayer Book.* And youth can read *Christian Social Witness* or *Horizons of Mission* before they do their mission projects. These books would also be useful for the last two years of the program (YAC), which encourages youth to take responsibility for their own spiritual formation.

If you do not use any curriculum or established program, the books of the series could form the basis of a youth church school class. Provide the books for the young people to read, but be realistic! The books are written for adults and will work better with some youth groups than others. Use your own judgment about which books would be best for your group.

The books in the series that we feel are most appropriate for youth are *Opening the Bible, Engaging the Word, Opening the Prayer Book, The Practice of Prayer, Living With History, Christian Social Witness,* and *The Anglican Vision.* If you use these books, put the emphasis on the questions that draw on their experience and connect that to information in the book. Use the activities as ways to engage them. Encourage them to ask questions and then guide them in finding the answers in the books. This lets them "lead" the direction of the class and gives them information in response to questions rather than "talking at" them about a topic. Listen, ask questions, and encourage thinking. You may be surprised to discover how much young people learn and how much they *want* to learn when they are engaged in the process.

～ Suggested Books for Ministry and Interest Groups

Congregations have a wide range of ministry and interest groups. Some of these groups have a specific task and may or may not meet regularly, while others exist primarily to meet. Any of them can incorporate study into their lives, although task-oriented groups may need to be persuaded of the value of this! Here are some suggestions to consider.

Church School Teachers and Children's Ministry Leaders

The volumes in the series are reference books that church school teachers ideally will read or at least become familiar with and use to obtain background material for specific lessons. They may also find some of the suggested questions and activities useful, especially with middle school children.

The series books are well suited to help congregations provide learning opportunities for those who are called to educate and form our children as Christians. You can invite church school teachers to read a book and meet once a month or so to discuss the book and how it relates to their teaching. This group can be led by the director of religious education, a clergyperson, or a member of the vestry. It is important that it be a time that supports those engaged in children's ministries. Remember to pray for them and their work and to affirm the importance of what they are doing. Giving them an opportunity to discuss these books helps them develop a deeper understanding of what they are teaching while forming a closer relationship with other teachers and congregational leaders.

Teachers usually will identify which books they are interested in or which ones apply most to what they are teaching. But, in general, the following books are good ones to start with: *The Anglican Vision, Opening the Bible, Engaging the Word, Opening the Prayer Book, The Practice of Prayer,* and *Living With History.*

Vestries and Mission Committees

Congregational governing boards will find the series books helpful both in regular meetings and for retreats. *The Anglican Vision* is a good choice for regular vestry or mission committee meetings. Begin each meeting with a half-hour dedicated to discussion of a chapter. It will take most of a year to get through just one book, but such study provides an excellent context for the governing board as they struggle with a variety of issues.

You can also use the books as a basis for vestry or mission committee retreats. One way to do this is to invite a team of two people to read and make a short presentation on a chapter and then lead the discussion. This spreads around the leadership responsibility, engages everyone in the process, and models collaborative leadership. It is also a good "warm-up" before inviting the vestry to lead the adult education group in reading and discussing the book.

When you are selecting a book to read, look at the crisis/short-term issues facing the governing board as well as the bigger picture and long-term issues. If you are facing significant changes in the congregation or community—and especially if those changes are creating discomfort—try *Living With History* and *Early Christian Traditions* as a way of putting the changes into a larger, historical context. Read *Horizons of Mission* if you are trying to discern the congregation's mission and future. If you are exploring service and outreach ministries or struggling with issues of injustice, read *Christian Social Witness* as a way to expand the focus of the discussion. If you are faced with a moral issue—anything from sexual misconduct, lying, theft, or disagreements over positions taken by the diocese, bishop, or national church—read *Ethics After Easter*.

If you want to deepen the spiritual life of the governing board, reading *The Practice of Prayer* or *Christian Wholeness* can focus the group on the role of prayer in their decision-making and leadership. If liturgical change of any sort is taking place, reading *A Theology of Worship* and *Opening the Prayer Book* will give board members the background and understanding of liturgy to help them lead and respond to other members of the congregation appropriately.

Lay Readers

Lay readers often receive little or no training and rarely meet as a group. Again, this is a missed opportunity for growth and leadership development. Many lay readers would benefit from reading *Opening the Prayer Book*, *A Theology of Worship*, *The Practice of Prayer*, and the two books on scripture, *Opening the Bible* and *Engaging the Word*. These books can help them become more knowledgeable about and aware of their role in the liturgy of the church.

It would be appropriate to ask the lay readers to meet monthly or weekly (perhaps as part of the adult education hour) to read and discuss these books

together. They can also use part of this time to practice reading the scriptures and giving each other feed-
back on their reading. Don't forget to include young
people—high school juniors and seniors who have
been in the *Journey to Adulthood* program are likely to
be well prepared to participate in such a group. If you
have a small church and no youth group activities or
if your older youth are "too busy" to be part of a
group, this is a good place for them to learn, be men-
tored by responsible adults, and contribute to the life
and mission of the congregation.

The liturgical leadership role of this group can be
expanded to provide formational leadership as well.
Since people see them functioning liturgically on
Sunday mornings, they naturally see them in a leadership role. Ask the lay readers to meet as a group to
read and discuss those five books and then work in
teams to initiate other programs in the congregation.

Lay Eucharistic Ministers

Apart from a short training in the diocese, lay
eucharistic ministers rarely receive training, support,
or spiritual direction in the congregation. This is a
missed opportunity for growth and can even be dan-
gerous. Lay eucharistic ministers are pastoral care
givers and, as such, need ongoing training, support,
and opportunities for spiritual growth. The Diocese of
Massachusetts has developed a lay eucharistic ministers training program that includes instructions for
ongoing support meetings.[6] Monthly supervision
meetings are important and several books in the series
can provide the focus for these meetings. For example,
The Practice of Prayer, *Opening the Bible*, *Engaging the
Word*, *Opening the Prayer Book*, *A Theology of Worship*,
Mysteries of Faith, and *Christian Wholeness* are logical
books for this group to read and discuss.

Pastoral Care Givers or Bereavement Care Givers
Congregations using the Stephen Ministry or other structured programs are likely to have ongoing training, support, and supervision processes already established. The books identified above for lay eucharistic ministers can appropriately be integrated into those existing group meetings. If you do not have a structured program but have laity engaged in pastoral care, you can easily include them in the group with the lay eucharistic ministers, as their ministries and concerns will be similar in nature.

Prayer Groups
There are a variety of prayer groups that may be present in a congregation. Some are not really groups—they are people on a list, a "prayer chain" who respond to requests for prayer. Some are groups that have a special focus, such as healing. Others meet regularly to learn about prayer or just to pray together. Most are based in the local congregation, but some are community-wide and others have national affiliations. For example, associates of various religious orders sometimes meet regionally and devotional groups, such as the rapidly growing Daughters of the King, provide contexts in which group members can meet to pray and form a rule of prayer. The Order of St. Luke focuses especially on the healing ministry.[7]

Prayer groups often include Bible study and/or book reading as part of their regular meetings. Obviously, *The Practice of Prayer* is a good first choice for this group. It also works well to focus on just one chapter per monthly meeting if your group chooses that meeting schedule. But this group is also likely to respond positively to *Christian Wholeness, Opening the Prayer Book, Mysteries of Faith, Opening the Bible,* and *Engaging the Word.*

Even if the group does not normally meet, it is useful to encourage them to meet for several weeks just once a year. In addition to the joint study of the book, the group can spend some time praying together for those who are on the congregation's prayer list and for their personal prayer concerns. This serves a couple of purposes. The shared time of prayer and study builds group cohesion and provides support and spiritual nourishment to those engaged in this ministry. It also is an excellent time to incorporate new members. Lent, for example, would be a good time for the group to meet and to invite others to learn about the ministry and perhaps consider it as their ministry. Another option is for the group to do this during a retreat. (See the section on retreats in chapter four for suggestions.)

Older Adults
Older persons are a valuable but overlooked ministry resource in a congregation. Because many of them have been involved in Christian education in the church for decades, we assume they are not interested in learning more. The opposite is often true: like all Christians, older adults seek a deeper relationship with God in Christ and want to learn more about the faith.

Any of the series books are appropriate for this group. If they do not express interest in any specific book, you might suggest *Opening the Bible* and *Engaging the Word* for groups that enjoy reflecting on the scriptures, or *The Practice of Prayer* for those who may be interested in learning about different forms of prayer. Most Episcopalians are familiar with forms of prayer in the prayer book—collects, intercessory prayer and liturgical prayer—and may believe that those are the only "approved" or "proper" ways to pray. It is not unusual to find life-long Episcopalians who have never heard of contemplative prayer, even though they may have developed this way of praying on their own many years ago.

Opening the Prayer Book and *A Theology of Worship* will help those facing liturgical changes, while *Living With History* and *Early Christian Traditions* are good choices for older adults who may be struggling with changes that are occurring in the church and in the world. And this group is likely to be more prepared to read and respond to *Mysteries of Faith* than other age groups: most have experienced mystery in their lives and have come to realize that there is much they can never truly understand but can still believe.

If you do not have a senior group, you might ask older adults in your congregation if they are interested in forming such a group. Older adults, especially if they live alone, might welcome an opportunity to gather during the week, perhaps for breakfast or lunch. They might also be willing to take the group meeting to an apartment complex or assisted living or nursing home facility so other older adults can participate.

Outreach Ministries

Outreach ministry groups will logically gravitate toward *Christian Social Witness* and *Horizons of Mission*, so those books are a good place to start. *Ethics After Easter* would be an interesting and challenging follow-up to that and/or *Living with History*, especially if the group is dealing with any of the movements addressed in the book (civil rights, women's movement, and so on).

Although it might not be their natural inclination, it is important to introduce this group to *Engaging the Word* and *The Practice of Prayer*, and to encourage them to incorporate prayer and scripture study into their regular meetings and work. Often outreach ministry group members "burn out" because they are so focused on "doing" that they neglect their own spiritual nourishment. The time spent in prayer, scripture reflection, and study ensures that these ministry groups are places for spiritual growth for the members as well as places where outreach ministry is planned, organized, and carried out.

Other Committees/Commissions

Most committees are task-focused and rarely include study as part of their agenda. There is, however, great benefit for them to incorporate faith formation into their committee work. This prevents the committee from becoming just another "job to do" and it provides a learning experience in a context that generally appeals to the interests of the group members.

Think about ways to incorporate the series books into various groups. For example, a stewardship, finance, or capital funds committee might read *Horizons of Mission* or *Christian Social Witness*. A communications committee might read *The Anglican Vision* as a way to help them think about what is unique about being Anglican and how that uniqueness can be incorporated into newsletters and other congregational communications.

Education committees might well read the entire series to help them understand the content of what a comprehensive education program for a congregation might be. They could use the series to help them evaluate curriculums, design education programs, and decide what educational offerings to provide. They could also recommend specific books to group leaders and church school teachers.

A liturgy/worship committee is likely to want to start with *Opening the Prayer Book* and *A Theology of Worship*, and would also find *Engaging the Word* and *The Anglican Vision* helpful in their work. *Early Christian Traditions* and *Living With History* can help set a context for liturgical change.

A search committee beginning the process of looking for a new rector also might read *The Anglican Vision* and *A Theology of Worship* to gain perspectives on what makes the Anglican Church and its worship unique. This might be especially important if you have several people from different denominational backgrounds on the search committee. Most of us unconsciously revert back to our childhood images of what we expect a clergyperson to be and those differing denominational expectations might confuse the process of looking for the rector of an Episcopal Church. Or, if your congregation has been affected by current changes in the church, they might read *Living With History* or *Ethics After Easter* as a way to gain perspective.

Altar Guilds
Altar guilds are more than just a cadre of folks willing to prepare for and clean up after worship services. This group rightly has the role of spiritual preparation for worship and thanksgiving afterward. Retreats or monthly meetings can focus on spiritual nurture and expanding their spiritual leadership role. Many altar guild members arrive early, whether they are on duty that Sunday or not, and spend the time before the service praying for the clergy and other worship leaders and the congregation. Likewise, they stay afterward to give thanks. This ministry has both a spiritual impact on the congregation and models an

approach to worship that invites others into a time of preparation and thanksgiving.

Four books, in particular, seem appropriate for use in helping altar guild members broaden their role. *The Anglican Vision, Opening the Prayer Book, A Theology of Worship*, and *The Practice of Prayer* can each be fruitfully read and discussed by the group. In addition to providing nurture to current members, retreats or monthly meetings are good times to invite potential members to join. Remember to include older adults—some of whom may have been members of the guild but are no longer able to carry out those tasks. Youth too can benefit from learning about and sharing in this group's ministry.

Choirs

Choirs probably are one of the most task-driven groups in the church. Partly this is because their task is clear and it is time-driven—the anthem must be ready for next Sunday! There are plenty of ways for choir directors to offer educational moments—relating a musical text to its scriptural roots, explaining words, phrases, or the theology behind the text, talking about the lessons appointed for the day and how the hymns relate to them or the season. A choir might have a retreat and use these books, but most choirs will not actually read and discuss them as part of choir rehearsal (although that would be an excellent educational experience). The director or individual members of the choir might read the books and look for places where they can offer information or perspectives that help choir members in their ministry.

It might be helpful to read *Opening the Prayer Book* and *A Theology of Worship*, especially the chapter on music and liturgy, to learn more about the liturgical leadership of the choir. *Opening the Bible* might provide information on reading and listening to the scriptures and *Engaging the Word* might help make connections between a musical text or hymn and the passages being read that Sunday. The choir might take time to learn how to reflect on the scriptures and spend a few moments discussing the next week's lessons prior to practicing the anthem. And *The Practice of Prayer* can help choir members develop a better sense of how they can provide prayer support before, after, and during the service as well as in their personal lives.

Renewal Ministries

A variety of renewal programs have been present in the church throughout its history. At the moment, Alpha is a very popular program that reaches the unchurched or people on the margins of the church. But what happens after the end of renewal programs or retreat experiences of this type? You have a group of people who often have had a "mountain-top experience" and who are now ready to become involved in the life of the congregation in a deeper way than before—or perhaps to become involved for the first time. Most people who have had a positive experience in programs such as this hope to continue the "high" they experienced and are disappointed when there is no place in the church where that seems possible.

In Alpha and most other renewal programs, small group discussion, personal sharing, personal prayer, and informal worship that includes simple, emotive songs are key elements, creating the intimacy and openness that enables people to be touched by a spiritual experience. A small group ministry such as Discipleship Groups (described under Small Group Ministry above) that includes the series books is a good next step. A small group ministry meets renewal participants where they are at the end of that experience and helps them move into deeper faith.

If you are instituting a small group ministry as a follow-up to a renewal experience, it is especially important that you pay attention to the key elements that will help these group members feel at home. Make sure you have a time of personal prayer—a time when people can pray for each other, can ask for prayers for specific concerns, and can pray about the topic being discussed as it relates to them. You might also find out which songs were favorites at their Alpha or renewal experience and use those as gathering songs at the beginning of the group session. And you might want to find a simple song of blessing to sing at the end—something like "God be with you 'til we meet again."

If possible, start the Discipleship Group immediately after Alpha or another renewal experience and try to keep participants in small groups with some (but not all) of the people from their former small groups. Encourage the participants to self-select into groups and suggest they might want to stay with some of their former participants but that they should also reach out to include some new members in their small group. This will allow groups that worked well to stay together while giving people who were in a group they did not like the opportunity to migrate to another group.

When you are looking for leaders for this group, you may want to approach some of the table leaders (Alpha has a team of people trained to lead discussions at each table) or encourage some of the group participants to lead. People who have been through a renewal experience are more accustomed to personal openness than the general Episcopalian might be. So leaders recruited from renewal event participants are more likely to ask the kind of discussion questions that "feel right" to those participants.

The goal is to provide a comfortable next step for participants in a renewal experience—a place that has at least some of the same elements present. At the same time, reading the books in this series will help those for whom their renewal experience is their "first love" experience in the church to deepen that love over time. The spiritual high that many experience in renewal programs and events is a valuable and sometimes even essential part of a person's spiritual formation. But prayerful study of the life, witness, theology, doctrine, and practices of the church and Christian faith are also important and essential. The point is to value both, and avoid the tendency to disparage either one or the other.

Men's Groups and Women's Groups

There are a variety of formal and informal gender groups. The most common of the formal groups are the Episcopal Church Women (ECW) and the Brotherhood of St. Andrew. In the past these were gender specific but in recent years most groups are open to both men and women.

The informal groups tend to be "home-grown"; that is, they were started at some time to meet a specific need and follow a format that is comfortable to the group. Examples of these groups include fellowship and work-related groups formed either by occupation or by members who work in a given neighborhood and gather for breakfast or lunch.

Most of these groups have an established program format and can easily use a book either as the content for the program or as background material for a presenter. They might want to coordinate with special projects or annual themes or, conversely, they might want to develop special projects or themes around the books. For example, an ECW or Brotherhood of St. Andrew group might declare a "Year of the Bible" and focus on *Opening the Bible* and *Engaging the Word* in their programs, sell Bibles as their annual fundraiser, or distribute Bibles as their annual outreach project. They might sponsor a "listen to the Bible" event—perhaps as an overnight retreat.[8] They might do some Bible-related events with the children or youth of the congregation, submit a Bible-related puzzle or quiz drawn from their study of these books for the monthly newsletter, or develop a weekly biblical "factoid" for the Sunday bulletin. This type of integration into a full-year program for a group moves the study of a book from just a discussion to looking at ways to apply it in real life.

	The Anglican Vision	Opening the Bible	Engaging the Word	The Practice of Prayer	Living With History	Early Christian Traditions	Opening the Prayer Book	Mysteries of Faith	Ethics After Easter	Christian Social Witness	Horizons of Mission	A Theology of Worship	Christian Wholeness
Adult Education Forums	■	■	■	■	■	■	■	■	■	■	■	■	■
Lenten Groups			■	■	■		■	■			■	■	■
Young Adult Groups	■	■	■	■			■		■			■	■
Bible Study Groups	■	■	■	■		■		■		■	■		■
Foyer Meetings	■												■
Small Group Ministry	■	■	■	■	■	■	■	■	■	■	■	■	■
Newcomers	■	■	■	■	■	■	■			■			■
Inquirers' Classes	■	■	■	■	■	■	■	■	■	■		■	■
Catechumenal Process	■	■	■	■	■	■	■	■	■		■	■	■
Youth Programs	■	■	■	■	■		■			■	■		■
Church School Teachers	■	■		■	■		■						
Vestries/Mission Committees	■					■	■		■	■	■	■	■
Lay Readers		■	■	■			■					■	

	The Anglican Vision	Opening the Bible	Engaging the Word	The Practice of Prayer	Living with History	Early Christian Traditions	Opening the Prayer Book	Mysteries of Faith	Ethics After Easter	Christian Social Witness	Horizons of Mission	A Theology of Worship	Christian Wholeness
Lay Eucharistic Ministries		■	■	■			■	■				■	■
Pastoral Care Givers		■	■	■			■	■				■	■
Prayer Groups		■	■	■			■	■					■
Older Adults		■	■	■	■	■	■	■				■	
Outreach Ministries			■	■	■				■	■	■		
Stewardship Committees										■	■		
Liturgy/Worship Committees	■		■	■	■	■	■	■	■	■	■	■	
Education Committees	■		■		■	■	■		■			■	■
Search Committees	■				■							■	
Altar Guilds	■			■			■					■	
Choirs		■	■	■			■					■	
Renewal Ministries	■	■	■	■	■	■	■	■	■	■	■	■	■
Men's & Women's Groups	■	■	■	■	■	■	■	■	■	■	■	■	■

Chapter Three

Establishing and Leading Groups

Once you have reviewed The New Church's Teaching Series and decided how you are going to use the books with which groups, it will be helpful to think about how you will recruit participants, organize the program, and lead the group. The following is designed to help those who have been designated as leaders for groups studying one or more of the books in the series.

~ Recruiting Leaders

If there is no established leader for the group, you will need to identify leaders. It is preferable to have at least two leaders—three if the group has more than fifteen people, and even more if you expect larger numbers. The ideal small group size is eight people. So if you expect thirty participants, you might have two team leaders who will manage the program and two small group leaders to assist with the four small groups.

We do not recommend that you *ask* for volunteers, especially the usual church announcement that pleads for someone—anyone—to please help. You can announce that the clergy or the education committee will be engaged in a discernment process to identify leaders for The New Church's Teaching Series. People who are interested in leading such groups may speak up and you can welcome them as part of the teaching team. However, do not automatically assume they can or should lead a group.

Asking for volunteers can lead to problems. First, it implies that leading this group is not an important ministry—after all, anyone can do it, and we do not care who volunteers, just so long as someone steps forward. Second, it puts you in a very awkward position if the only volunteer is someone who is inappropriate or ineffective. You will rapidly kill any enthusiasm for an education program if you allow poor leadership simply because someone volunteered and you did not feel you could say no. And it is extremely difficult to say no to someone when you begged for a volunteer!

Ask people you trust can do the job. Better yet, engage in a serious discernment process: meet with a small group of people to identify what you need in group leaders, review the entire congregational list, and covenant to pray daily for guidance during the next week or two. Then meet again and share your thoughts. Create a "long list" of several possibilities and adjourn for another week of prayer. Finally, meet and decide whom you will ask. Send one or two representatives of the group to invite them to be part of the leadership team, explaining why you are asking them. Ask them not to respond immediately but rather to join you in another week of prayer. Call them a week later for their answer. Accept whatever answer they give (no fair trying to change their minds) and thank them. Congregations that have used this system of identifying group leaders for a variety of ministries usually have greater success because it is a spiritually grounded process and it communicates the importance of the ministry of leadership.

Finally, make sure you give your leaders the support they need to do the job. This chapter is designed to help them. But, in addition, make experienced leaders available to talk about group leadership or to sit in the group and mentor a new leader. Provide any resources that will be needed—newsprint, markers, videos. Have the meeting room ready. Provide refreshments. And remember to pray for the leaders and thank them for their work.

~ Recruiting Participants

The traditional way of inviting people to a group is to put a notice into the Sunday bulletin. This is a start, but not adequate since it will primarily attract core congregation members who tend to come to whatever is offered by the church. If you want to expand participation it is important to expand your communications effort. The best way to recruit participants is to invite people personally. This may not be easy, especially if you are shy, do not know many people, or are part of a large congregation. But there are a variety of ways you can accomplish this.

Begin by identifying your target audience. Who are the people most likely to be interested in this book? Whom do you want to invite into a deeper relationship with the congregation? What types of people do you feel have not been served by other educational offerings? What ministry groups do you want to engage in learning more? There are many potential target audiences. You will want to pick one or, at most, two types of people to focus on. This will allow you to make a general invitation and still reach out to some specific people.

Once you have identified your target audience, talk with the congregation's clergy about who fits into that group and what needs they might have. This will have an impact on your planning and how you present your invitation. For example, if your target group has many young families, you will want to arrange child care and, if you are meeting in the evening, a family meal. This will then be part of your invitation.

Include an announcement about your group in all advance mailings—the newsletter, your educational opportunities brochure, posters on the bulletin boards, and so on. These should announce events about four to six months before the program starts. About three Sundays before you begin, make an announcement during church services, indicating that you will be at the back of the church afterward to field questions. Recruit your team leader, assisting clergy, members of the education committee, and people who have already signed up for the group to help you.

After the service has concluded, position yourselves just beyond the clergyperson (who will be busy greeting congregants) and give each interested person who approaches you a flyer or brochure with a description of the group and the book the group will discuss. Make sure to include information on when and where the group will meet. If you are recruiting people who are not regulars in your education program (newcomers, parents who drop their children off at church school and leave, marginal attendees), keep the number of meetings to less than eight sessions. Most potential participants in this category will not sign up for long programs. As you hand each person an invitation, remember to invite them personally yourself! For instance, "Here's some information about the group learning about *The Book of Common Prayer.* We'd love to have you join. Can I answer any questions you might have?" "No questions? Would you like to be part of the group?" If the answer is "yes" continue: "Let me add your name to our list of participants. I look forward to seeing you." If the answer is "no" or, more likely, "I'll think about it," continue: "I hope you will come; I'd love to have you as part of the group. Please feel free to call me if you have any questions. My number is on the information sheet I gave you." (Be sure to include a phone number on the flyer for people to call with questions!)

Because many people will be going by, you need to have several people ready to do this. Make sure you review with them what they are to say or most of them will just pass out the paper without comment. The piece of paper is there for two reasons: 1) to give you a way to start the conversation, and 2) to give the person something in writing to look at later.

Then, two weeks after the first announcement of the sessions, repeat the invitation. Before and after church approach specific people you would like to have as part of the group and say that you want to issue a personal invitation to them to join the group. Include a reason that is sincere:

- "I'd like to get to know you better"; or,
- "The group already has lots of other young mothers and would be a way for you to build a support network"; or,
- "I'm making a point of inviting a number of people who are new to the congregation because I think it will be a good way for you to meet each other and learn about the church as well."

You can also send people a written invitation to join the group. A brief handwritten note does better than a computer-generated letter. However, if you do send a printed letter, make sure you sign it personally and, if possible, add a one-sentence personal greeting. And, of course, you can call people at home to invite them.

The last communications task is to send a letter to everyone who signed up to remind them of the time and place, reiterate what you will be doing, and express your pleasure that they are joining the group. On the first week, make sure you have signs in the halls both to remind people and to invite others into the group.

Some of this will not be necessary in a small congregation (under one hundred average attendance), but larger congregations have fewer links between people and need personal invitations and reminders to help "glue" a new group together. Most of us complain about the fact that the same individuals always come to everything, but we are unwilling to do the work involved in getting new people, or those on the margins, involved. In today's busy world, with a multitude of activities competing for everyone's attention, it is essential that churches intentionally invite people and not assume that a bulletin announcement will do the job.

✌ Understanding How Adults Learn

While some groups may include children or youth, most of the books in the series will be read and discussed in adult groups. Before you plan what you will do in your group, it is important that you understand a few basics about how adults learn.

The most important characteristic is that *adults learn by doing*. It is thought that adults learn about 10 percent of what they read (books, handouts); 20 percent of what they hear (lectures, sermons); 30 percent of what they see (newsprint, pictures, graphs); 50 percent of what they hear and see (videos); 70 percent of what they hear and say (discussion); and 90 percent of what they say and do (role-plays, activities). This is why reading a book *and* discussing it with others is such an effective way for adults to learn about a subject and remember what they learned, and why activities can make that learning experience even more effective. By making the series books an educational program you move people from learning at about the 10 percent level to the 90 percent level.

The second characteristic is that adults learn best when they *integrate what they are learning into their lives.* This means making connections between the information and each person's life experience. A couple of common ways to do this are to ask questions that encourage people to make those connections, and to create experiences in which they make the connections. Invite participants to draw a picture, write a poem or hymn, create a drama, or engage in role-play. All of these invite people to move away from just thinking about content toward applying it to real life.

Finally, adults learn best when they *do something with what they learned.* In other words, we learn best when what we have learned changes how we live and move and have our being. You can encourage this by inviting participants to commit themselves to one thing that incorporates what they learned into their daily lives or into their Bible reading or into how they worship.

These characteristics about adult learning speak directly to how you lead the group. And they make your job easier! You are not responsible for making people learn—only they can do that for themselves. Nor are you responsible for knowing everything (or even anything) about the topic at hand. Rather, you are responsible for creating a learning environment. This means giving people access to information (in this case the books have all or most of that) and setting up ways for them to engage that material and incorporate it into their lives.

∿ Creating a Learning Environment

There are several very simple things you can do to facilitate learning. The first one concerns room arrangement. If at all possible, set up chairs in a circular pattern rather than in rows facing the front. You can either include the leaders in the circle or, if you need to use newsprint, make the circle more of a "U" shape and put the newsprint easel in the opening of the "U." If your role is to make a brief presentation and ask questions, you can do that seated in the circle.

These room arrangements communicate the collaborative nature of learning. The traditional model of chairs in a row communicates that you have something you will deliver to the participants. "I know, you don't; I tell, you listen." Setting up the room in the traditional fashion will create demands on you as a leader to know and tell and will discourage participation. Putting chairs in a circle encourages participation and interaction among the participants.

The second step you can take concerns hospitality. We encourage you to serve refreshments, especially if the meeting is longer than 45 minutes. If it is after church, your congregation may provide coffee in another room and participants may be used to picking up their drink and bringing it to the meeting room. Think about whether this really works well or whether is encourages people to straggle in late or not show up at all because they have been caught in conversations in the other room. In many cases it is better to set up a refreshment table in your meeting room.

Give some care to the refreshment table and the general appearance of your room. These are honored guests—think of them like Mary, seated at Christ's feet, eager to learn. Congregations often allow church meeting rooms to become messy and unattractive. Take the time to put a small vase of flowers on the refreshment table. Think about an appropriate picture or perhaps an icon that you can add to the table or as a focal point somewhere in the room. Or, for example, if you are studying a book about the Bible, put a low coffee table in the center of the circle and display an assortment of Bibles there, along with a couple of candles. Create a poster with an appropriate saying. Look around the church: you might be surprised to find pictures, statues, books, vestments, or other beautiful items that you can temporarily move into your room. This can help create a welcoming atmosphere and may also let people see that object in a new light. Often we pass by a picture that has been in the hallway for years without even seeing it.

Think about what your participants will need. Are they likely to want to take notes or are you asking them to write down their thoughts before discussing them? If so, place a pen and a pad of paper on each chair before participants arrive, with extras available. Are you sure that all participants know each other by name? If not, provide name tags and make sure you are wearing one too. Will the group be breaking into several smaller groups? If so, make sure you have group leaders scattered around the circle so they can easily gather their group. If you will be moving the small groups to other rooms, check to see that those rooms are ready for them and that each group leader knows where to go.

Finally, establish group norms at the outset. You can write those you propose on a sheet of newsprint and ask the group to add others. Post that newsprint in a conspicuous place for the duration of your meeting. You might want to include such items as:

- Everyone's input is welcome.
- We assume that none of us is an expert or has all of the answers—all of us have something to learn.
- We will listen to and respect each other even if we don't agree with each other.
- We will actively seek to ensure that everyone has an opportunity to speak.
- We will read each chapter before the meeting time.
- We will focus our discussion on the topic at hand and follow the group agenda.
- We will begin and end on time unless we renegotiate the starting and ending times.
- We will not smoke in the meeting room.
- We will help ourselves to refreshments as needed and take breaks at agreed times.

Begin your first meeting by welcoming people and reviewing these norms. Invite the group to add any they might want to propose. Then ask the group if they are willing to live by these norms for the duration of the group. Finally, review the schedule so everyone knows what to expect and can be prepared for it.

〜 Sizing the Group

If you have less then twelve participants, you can meet in one group. Once you get to twelve or so, it becomes increasingly difficult to facilitate the group and, more importantly, participants cannot have enough "air time" per person for them to feel they are active participants in the group. Therefore, it is best to break into smaller groups. The ideal group size is about eight participants. Remember to designate how many participants will be in each group, who the leaders are, and where the small groups are to meet. Ideally, you want to stay in the same meeting room, as travel time increases greatly once you let them out of the door! Somehow a 30-second walk to the next room turns into a 7-minute "got to go to the bathroom, get another cup of coffee, or discuss what someone was doing/wearing" break.

If you break into smaller groups you will need someone to facilitate each small group. If you are team leading this, each of you can take one group. If you need additional groups, ask participants you know to be good discussion leaders to stand ready to take up that role. It is best to have a couple of extra people ready to jump in if needed during the first week or two until you know how many participants the group will have. You might want to give each of them a copy of this guide and direct them to this chapter on leading groups for a refresher. Explain that they do not need to prepare, they just need to help the group select and focus on the provided questions, solicit questions the group members might have, and encourage everyone to participate equally. Their only other responsibility is to meet with you after the session if they have problems in their session (for example, someone who dominates, puts down others, pontificates, or presumes to be an expert, or noise or temperature problems in the room). That will give you an opportunity to brainstorm ideas about how to handle the problem.

If you have a large group (twenty-five or more) or if you have plenty of small group facilitators it is best to have at least one of the team leaders free to wander about. This person's role is to make sure all is going well and to help with timekeeping.

∽ Leadership Styles

There are a variety of ways to structure the leadership of a group and a number of leadership styles that can be adopted for various situations. For example, a *didactic* leadership style is likely to be less helpful because it makes the leader an expert on the subject who then "teaches" (talks about) what he or she knows. The learners take notes and often are tested for recall. This lecture style is one that does not work especially well for adult learning, so we do not recommend it. Besides that, it requires a great deal of work on your part!

The *facilitator* leadership style is one in which the leader guides the participants in learning about the topic. The primary responsibility is to provide some introductory information and then guide the discussion. An understanding of group process and an ability to ask questions is important. This is the leadership style that will usually work best for a wide range of adult education programs.

You can lead the group by yourself. Or, another alternative is *shared leadership* in which two or more people lead the group. This is helpful in that one leader will be observing the group and can often identify someone who is trying to get into the discussion or can remember a point that needed to be made but was forgotten by the leader speaking at the time. It also means you have a backup for the times when one leader cannot attend. Small group leaders can also be part of a leadership team and sometimes one person will take responsibility for logistics (room arrangement, refreshments). The other advantage of shared leadership is that it is a good way to develop new leaders. Shared leadership does take more planning time, as the entire team needs to know what will happen and who will lead what portions of the session. But the benefits of shared leadership often outweigh that cost.

It is possible for these groups to be *self-led* or to use *rotating leadership*. This works best with an established group that is used to working together. Usually a different person takes the primary leadership role each week. In some groups, the group members all take responsibility for asking the questions, encouraging each other to speak, summarizing, and so on. This can be very effective provided that a sizable portion of the group has the ability and willingness to take on these active roles. If not, silence or idle chatter tends to emerge.

Finally, a word about clergy roles in discussion groups. A clergyperson may be the group leader or, preferably, part of a leadership team. Or a priest or deacon may simply attend that group. What is important is that the clergy do not take on the role of expert, or get pulled into the dominant role. Often this can be avoided by being in the facilitator role, where the clergy ask the questions. Their knowledge of the subject means they are often in a good position to pose questions that encourage the group members to think about and work with the material in the book.

~ Group Development

Groups have a life with a beginning, an end, and identifiable stages of group life in between. Having some basic understanding of those dynamics can help a group leader respond appropriately to what is happening in the group. The four stages of group life are:

> *Forming:* Who belongs to this group? What do I have to do to belong and be accepted? What will we do together?

Storming: Who has the power in this group? Whose opinion counts? What happens if I challenge the leaders (formally or informally)?

Norming: How will we work together? What "rules" (norms) will guide our behavior?

Performing: Now that we've settled all of that, we can really get down to work!

A group can get "stuck" in one place if the leader does not recognize what is happening and does not help the group move through that stage. The first stage (Forming) is helped by doing introductions (who belongs?), setting norms, naming what the group will do and how it will be led, and so on. It is generally an easy stage to recognize and move through. However, if you fail to do introductions or let people know what will happen, you will find that it takes the group several sessions before they move to the next stage.

The second stage (Storming) tends to make leaders uncomfortable. But it is much easier if you know that all groups rebel or have some conflict and that this is necessary and helpful to group life. The behaviors you see at this stage include people turning to the clergyperson for leadership when he or she is not the designated leader; a dominant person will start to take over the group; someone will challenge the leader; or someone will break one of the group norms.

None of these behaviors are malicious or even intentional. It is simply a part of group process. Like teenagers, members of a group need to push against the boundaries just to see where they are. The most important thing the leader can do is be a "non-anxious presence." In other words, stay calm and look like you are in control, even if you do not know what is happening! The worst-case scenario is when the leader and a group member or members get into an argument over who is right or who is wrong. The leader's role is to reassert the norms ("We will listen to and respect each other even if we don't agree") and to ask questions that invite others to offer their opinion.

The leader needs to continue to be the leader. It is tempting to give in to a strong person who begins to dominate the discussion (especially if it is a clergyperson), but by calmly staying in the leadership role, facilitating the participation of other members of the group, and, if necessary, asking the dominator to hold his or her comments so others can speak, the leader provides a safe space for the group to work within. That is one of the leader's primary tasks: to create a place where everyone can speak and be heard, where everyone can explore ideas, where everyone can ask questions. If you let any one person take over the group, the rest of the group loses the opportunity to grow and learn.

At the third stage (Norming) the group begins to be productive. Everyone has figured out how the group works and what the norms are. When norms need to be changed, that is openly stated and dealt with promptly. The group is cohesive and lots of ideas and information flows freely.

From the third stage, the group usually progresses with little effort to the fourth stage (Performing). Now the group members trust each other and subgroups, pairs, and individuals can carry out tasks on the group's behalf. The group's work is clear, collaborative working relationships have been established, and the group responds positively to any changes required.

⁓ Starting a Session

Each book in the series provide a number of resources to assist you in planning your session. Each book concludes with a list of questions for group discussion—

several for every chapter in each book. These are a good place to begin. Most of the books also include a resource section that lists additional books and audio-visual materials relevant to that book. We especially encourage you to look for appropriate videos, as they can often be effectively used to launch a group or to interject extra energy into a group midway through a book. Contact your local diocesan or ecumenical resource center for suggestions. The Center for the Ministry of Teaching at Virginia Seminary has a variety of videotapes available to congregations. Another good resource is the Episcopal Media Center (formerly The Episcopal Radio/TV Foundation), which has video-tapes and audiotapes available for purchase or rental.[1]

You may also want to identify speakers who can serve as a keynoter for the first session or can bring expertise to a particular topic addressed by the book. Panel discussions are also an effective way to highlight a chapter—especially if you have several people in the congregation or community that have expertise or a special interest in the subject matter. Don't forget to consider other ways of starting a session—try a role-play, a reading, or a "debate" with assigned positions, for example.

Whether you have a shorter or longer time-frame, it is best to keep the introductory part relatively short. The rumor is that the adult attention span is thirteen minutes—and that may be overly optimistic! Aim for brief input at the beginning, just to get people on board and focused on the topic. Then engage them in discussion and/or an activity that enables them to work with the material. Remember that adults learn best when they are doing something active—talking, writing, acting, and so on. So the goal for the start-up time is to motivate the group to move to learning at a deeper level.

～ Leading a Discussion

One of the best ways to start a discussion, nurture it, direct it, and help people learn something from it is by asking good questions. In most situations you will find the questions for each chapter of the books invaluable as the starting point for your discussion. Do not feel you must use all of them, but read them and envision how your group might respond to them. In some cases you may want to take notes on pages in the book that related to that question or identify other resources that address it.

Look at the types of questions listed below and jot down a couple of follow-up questions for each question in the book. Then develop several questions that might be specific to your group or your congregation, or might connect to the prior week's discussion. Go into the group with a list of at least one question for every five minutes of discussion time. You may never need them all, but it is always best to have more questions than you need! And if you run out of questions, you can always ask people for their questions—in fact, it is good to do that along the way rather than just at the end.

There are many different types of questions, each useful for a different purpose and in a different setting.[2]

- Yes or no questions
- Short information questions
- Storytelling or reporting questions
- Expansion questions
- Feeling or experience questions
- Relational questions
- Processing questions
- Application questions
- Evaluative questions

Yes or no questions are just what they say. They only require one-word answers and thus are show-stoppers. Avoid this type of question if you want to get a discussion going. Use it for things like renegotiating time: "Do you want to stay another ten minutes?"

Short information questions are just one step from yes or no questions. They ask for information like name, address, or job. In a discussion, they are most useful as "warm-up" questions at the beginning of a new group or session. For example, it is helpful to have each person say his or her name and one other item of information at the start of a new group. The fact that they have spoken once makes it easier for most people to speak again.

Storytelling or reporting questions invite people to tell about an experience they have had. This might be a story about their past, or it might be a report on the small group experience they have just completed.

Expansion questions build on a story, report, or comment someone has already contributed: "Could you tell us more about that?" These questions encourage the speaker to continue. They are especially useful with group members who are a bit reticent and may offer extremely brief remarks. These questions are also useful when the group is well established and the leader wants to get them to talk more and be less dependent on the leader.

Feeling or experience questions encourage the speaker to focus on personal reactions to the material being discussed. These questions are more personal and probing; they can be felt as intrusive unless a trust relationship has been built. It is usually best not to use these types of questions in the first few hours of a group's life. When group members spontaneously begin saying how they felt about this or that, it is a good clue that they are ready for this type of question.

Relational questions encourage the speaker to relate what he or she just said to something said previously or to some other topic. For example: "How is (this problem) related to (previous problem, another situation)?"

Processing questions are designed to help people understand the significance or meaning of something or to learn from it. They encourage people to reflect on and make sense of an experience or information they have received.

Application questions help people take what they have learned in one setting and apply it to another. They are best used after a group has discussed a topic or experience, reflected on it, and identified what it meant to them and/or named something they learned from it. You can then ask how they will apply what they learned to future situations that are similar to or different from the one discussed.

Evaluative questions ask people to evaluate an experience—usually an experience they just completed: "How was this session for you?" "What suggestions do you have for improvements?" It is useful to ask these questions at the end of a session and essential at the last meeting of the group—though many people will prefer to give a written evaluation at the end.

Remember also to include processing and application questions toward the end of each session. You may want to add a session at the very end just to focus on processing and applying what people have learned.

~ Managing Time and People

One of the roles of a leader is to manage the time and agenda. Begin promptly at the established time. If you start three minutes late this week, the majority of the group will begin to show up later next week. And if you then adjust to starting five or ten minutes late, they will show up a couple of minutes after that! So the solution is to start on time. The latecomers will usually adjust to that in a week or two and others will also be more prompt.

It is also important to end on time. If you are in the middle of a discussion, you can either announce that those who want to stay on are welcome to do so or you can ask the group if they would like to stay for another ten minutes. If this happens consistently, you can ask the group if they want to renegotiate the ending time and extend it by fifteen minutes or so.

The other timing issue is moving the group from one point in the agenda to another. Plan ahead and allocate estimated minutes to each agenda item. Then watch the time and begin moving the group to the next agenda item when that time arrives. You can make adjustments as you go along, but avoid getting bogged down on one item. It is easy for dominant people to capture the group and talk endlessly about a specific point. Once you feel that the comments are getting repetitive or are not adding anything new, move the group to the next item.

In this type of group, you will most likely begin with an agenda. In fact, we have suggested an outline for you. Once you have done one or two books with the same group (or essentially the same group), you might want to ask them if the agenda you are using meets their needs or if they want to try a different way of doing things. You can always try another way of ordering your time together and then see if the group finds that helpful or not. If not, try something else!

Probably the most challenging part of group leadership is managing people—especially "difficult" people. The following is a discussion of several types of disruptive behaviors and some actions a leader can take to address them. Normal courtesy and gentle questions that invite people to talk about some aspect of the book often gets the discussion started. But inevitably some difficulties arise that you, as the leader, need to guard against: hogging, bogging, and frogging.

Hogging: Make sure that everyone gets their fair share of air time—don't let one or two people monopolize the conversation.

Bogging: Keep the group from getting stuck in one place in a low energy, listless discussion—make sure the group moves briskly forward with fun and excitement.

Frogging: Stay on course, sticking to the task instead of wandering all over so that people get lost.

In all cases you can state the applicable norm(s) so that all members of the group can take responsibility for group. If you have a *hogger* or two in your group, you can:

• Suggest a maximum of one minute speaking time, and have someone keep time—for example, the dominant individual.

• Sit next to over-talkers.

• Ask everyone to give a word, phrase, or just one sentence in response to a question.

• Speak directly to the over-talker (after the session) and encourage that person to help you by drawing others into the conversation, asking them to comment, or by asking questions.

If your group is *bogging down,* you can:

• Take a break (if your group time is more than an hour).

• Introduce a new subject.

• Ask each person to turn to a partner and discuss the next question and then share responses with the whole group.
• Break into small groups for the next question.
• Introduce an activity that gets people up and moving.
• If the heat is putting people to sleep, open the windows or turn up the air conditioning!

If your group is *frogging,* you can:
• Consistently return to the topic by asking the question a second or third time, slightly rewording it.
• Gently interrupt a consistent frogger and ask the person to relate the gist of their comment to the topic or question at hand or ask the person to hold that comment aside and refocus on the topic.
• Summarize the group's discussion to this point before asking another question.
• Ask the group to summarize and say where the discussion is.
• State the obvious—that the group is off track—and invite them to refocus.
• Ask people to hold comments about X and say when that topic will be covered. This is especially useful when the group gets ahead of the agenda.

An easier issue of people management is incorporating newcomers. While it may be easy, it is often forgotten. When you notice a new member, start that session by welcoming the person and having people introduce themselves. Briefly summarize what you have covered so far—directing these comments to the group, not the new person (so that person doesn't feel singled out for this "instruction"). One small group leader should be prepared to invite the newcomer into his or her group. You can establish that person ahead of time ("You take this week's new person and I'll take next week's") or it can simply be that the person sitting nearest the newcomer will initiate the invitation.

~ Activities

Most adults learn more and remember more if they are actively engaged with the material rather than listening to someone talk about it. Activities are especially important for "kinetic learners"—those people who learn best by physically doing something.

Activities are also important in the group process. They can serve several functions:

- An initial activity can attract people to the group and create interest in the topic.
- An activity during the group's life can revive flagging interest, interject new perspectives into a group that is bogged down, or build group cohesion.
- An activity at the end of a group's life can sum up the experience and help participants apply it to daily life.

Activities require advance planning and careful thought about logistics, materials, and timing. This is a good time to recruit some helpers who can handle some of the details and, if you are inexperienced, help you develop a realistic plan.

Think about the amount of space you will need to do the activity and work out a detailed list of what materials you will need. Remember to think about different people's needs: Will some group members need chairs to sit on? Does anyone need wheelchair access? Is the lighting going to be adequate for people to see well enough to write? Do you need to provide props? What kind of supplies will be required? It is usually best to have more of what you think you need, rather than less.

Then think about how you will get people from point A to point B: Do you need cars, guides, maps? Even moving people from one room to another can be a challenge! It is usually best to give very clear directions and have a leader for each small group who will, immediately after the directions are given, stand up and move promptly to point B, urging participants to follow. And it is important that your leaders begin the activity promptly when they get there. This encourages people to move to the destination without taking multiple detours or chatting with their friend along the way. If you do not start promptly, you will, most likely, run out of time.

Think about how you will inspire the group to get started on the activity. This is especially important if the activity is something unfamiliar. You might want to recruit a couple of people who will immediately jump in and start doing whatever is suggested, setting an example for others. The leaders will also want to do the activity whenever that is feasible (that is, when they are not required to be giving directions along the way). Again, that sets an example and gets the group moving. As leader you should never ask a group to do anything (or answer any question) you are not willing to do yourself.

Finally, think about how you will end the activity. Keep an eye on the time and communicate the time to the group ("We only have about five minutes left to finish our project"). If the activity is taking far more time than you anticipated and the group is engaged in the project, it can be held over for the next session. Five to ten minutes before the end of the session, stop the action and note that there does not seem to be enough time to finish up. Suggest how far the group could go in this session and ask the group if they want to stay an additional X minutes to finish or if they want to continue at the next session.

～ Session Closure and Integration Time

One of the most important aspects of a session is how we end. Often the ending time is reached and the group hastily concludes with everyone dashing off while the last couple of people are still discussing the issue. This way of ending hampers the learning process.

Watch your time carefully and five minutes before the ending time, stop the group's work and invite participants to reflect on what they have learned. Simply stating what people learned helps them remember it. Ask them what was new, or exciting, or disturbing to them. Ask how people relate what they learned to other aspects of their lives or how they might use it in their lives. Ask how it applies to the congregation. Ask them what difference it makes. The goal of these few minutes is to encourage participants to reflect on the experience and integrate that experience into their lives. Dashing off without a conscious time of reflection usually means that what people learned dashes out of their minds just as quickly!

～ Ending a Group

We often have difficulty saying "goodbye" and that is reflected in our tendency to end the last session of the group by just dissolving—going out "not with a bang but a whimper." Take time to ask the participants to say what they have learned during in the group as part of the evaluation. Thank everyone for their participation. Announce the topic of the next group and say when and where it will be meeting. Distribute a brief written summary of the next topic. Invite people to attend—if you are doing an ongoing series, you can even have a sign up sheet for them to register immediately. Close with a prayer giving thanks for the wisdom and learning God has enabled.

✌ Working With an Existing Group

When using The New Church's Teaching Series with existing groups, such as prayer groups or vestries, you will need to renegotiate how the group works together. Invite the group to try a new agenda (or a modification they suggest) for at least three meetings and then reassess. Make sure you point out how this study relates to the work of the group and why it is important to do.

If the study session takes up a significant amount of the group's normal meeting time, suggest extending the meeting time by fifteen minutes or so. You can also review the work the group does and reallocate it over a longer period of time. However, most groups will find that if they covenant both to study and work, the work will still get done in the remaining time. Remember, work expands to fill the time available and most church groups are highly inefficient. Encourage them to find ways to do their work more efficiently so they can fit this important study time into their group's schedule.

If there are group members who are definitely not interested in studying a book together, set a time for study and a time for business, thus allowing those people to come for the business session only. Stick to the time schedule and take a five-minute break between the end of the study time and the start of the business time. Start the business session with a brief summary of what the study time discussed and what was learned in it. Occasionally invite those group members who are not part of the study session to join—remind them they are welcome at any time.

∽ Administration and Finance

Finally, a word about how to order the books, pay for them, and what to do with them afterward. You can order the books from your local bookstore or directly from Cowley Publications, but do it well ahead of the first session.

Even if your congregation has a large enough budget to pay for the books, we encourage you to charge or suggest a donation from participants. People value what they pay for. Set up a table with a sign indicating the cost of the book and a smaller note that says, "Donations of any amount accepted." People can then pay what they can afford.

If your congregation does not have enough funds to order books before you know how many people will attend, you will need to move your recruitment schedule ahead and take "orders" from participants, collecting funds ahead of time.

If you have some church members who are financially able, you can set up an education or library fund for classes based on The New Church's Teaching Series, and invite people to contribute to it. If you are a small church with limited funds and have a significant number of people with limited income, consider partnering with a larger congregation in your diocese. They may be willing to "recycle" some of the books they have already used in their program. Again, ask for assistance but encourage each participant to pay something, even if it is a small amount.

Another way to generate funds to purchase the books is simply to ask the vestry or mission committee. Adult education often has a meager budget, or no

budget at all. Make the case for why funds are needed. Or ask a group in the congregation to help raise
funds for this purpose. You could even ask the clergy
to take a special offering to start The New Church's
Teaching Series Fund.

Finally, don't forget your diocese. Some dioceses
have funds for such purposes or can suggest ways
you can obtain funds to help you purchase the books.

Chapter Four

Various Formats for Using the Books

There are five primary settings in which to use the series books:
- Sunday morning education groups (usually 45-minute sessions)
- Afternoon or evening education sessions (usually about 2 hours)
- Incorporation into existing groups and programs (variable time available)
- Retreats (usually one to three days)
- Conferences (usually one to three days)

Each congregation and each situation within your congregation will be best served by a different time frame and format. Think about your situation and select a format that fits your situation or best meets your needs. Then plan what you will do during the time available. The following pages outline a 45-minute session, a 2-hour session, a retreat, and a conference format. Obviously these are generic templates that you will need to adapt to your individual circumstances. They are designed to give you a basic format that you can use as a springboard from which to develop your own plan.

⁓ Suggested 45-Minute Session
Materials Needed
- A copy of the book being discussed for each participant
- An easel with newsprint, markers, and masking tape for the leaders
- A room where chairs can be arranged in a circle or semicircle
- Refreshments

Optional Materials (include if needed in a particular session)
- A Bible for each participant
- A copy of *The Book of Common Prayer* for each participant
- Newsprint, markers, and masking tape for each small group
- Music and a CD player or cassette player
- VCR and TV

Gathering Time:
5-10 minutes (before the announced session time)
Set up refreshments and the room so everything is ready at least 15 minutes before the announced session time. Hospitality is important—make sure the table is inviting and that people are welcomed as they arrive. If you like, you can add fresh flowers to the table and/or soft music in the background as people gather. Provide name tags if the group is large or the group members do not know each other, especially if you have opened the group to the community.

Starting the Session:
5 minutes

Introductions (first session)

Introduce the leaders and invite each participant to say their name. If you want them to say more than that, you will need to schedule an extra session unless you only have about eight to ten participants. Even ten participants taking a minute each will more than double this gathering time.

A good alternative is to have the first session focus entirely on introductions. Break a large group into several groups of about six participants each and invite people take 20 minutes to say who they are, what they hope to gain, and what they fear might happen or not happen in the group. Ask each small group to record their group's "hopes and fears" (without attribution) and report them back to the larger group. Take the last 10 minutes or so to describe what you have planned and check to see if that meets their expectations or if you need to make some adjustments going forward. This is an especially useful way to begin if a significant number of people do not know one another and you, as the leaders, do not know them.

An opening prayer

Resist the temptation to merely rattle through a collect from the prayer book. This is an opportunity to model praying (versus reading a prayer). The traditional Episcopal greeting and response—"The Lord be with you," "And also with you"—is very useful in letting everyone know what is going to happen. But then pause for several seconds to allow yourself and others to become aware of God's presence. When you feel ready, *pray* the collect you have selected or offer a prayer of your own. The reason you are starting with prayer is to ask God to be active in the session and to help people become aware that God is an active participant. So this is not just a formality—it is a means of being present to God, a way of attending to God's place and role in our lives.

Introducing the Session:
5-10 minutes
Summarize the chapter in your own words or use some other way to introduce the material (see the section on Starting a Session in chapter three for suggestions). In your introduction you might cover the major points the author makes and include several brief comments about your own reaction to the text. Look at the questions the group will be discussing for ideas about which points are most likely to engender conversation. Do not answer the question for the group, but share your own thoughts and feelings. For example: "The author presents idea X, which I found a totally new way of looking at this. I had always assumed Y, but am I now rethinking how I look at this question." Another way to engage people is to voice the questions and concerns that the chapter raised for you. Again, do not answer the questions, just ask them and encourage others who might also have questions to raise them in the group discussion.

Discussing the Chapter:
25-30 minutes (including 5 minutes "travel time")
At this point, large groups of more than ten or twelve people will break into smaller groups in order to begin the discussion questions. Be sure to designate how many participants will be in each group, who the leaders are, and where the small groups are to meet.

If you have developed questions of your own, distribute them at this time. Suggest they start with the question that they are most attracted to, disturbed by, or energized by rather than just taking them in order. After they have spent 5 to 10 minutes on that question, they can select another question on the list and proceed with discussing that one.

It is usually helpful to assign the role of timekeeper to one of the team leaders. This person can then remind the groups when they have about 2 minutes left to wrap up their discussion. Make sure you get them moving at least 7 minutes before the close of the session or they will not have time for closure.

Closure:
5 minutes

Gather everyone together and ask: "What did you learn today?" "What was most important, exciting, or new to you? Give me your *Reader's Digest* version"—a very short answer, just a few words. Take about 2 minutes worth of responses unless there is great energy and many people want to talk; if so, let this run the entire 4 minutes.

If or when the energy flags, ask: "How do you think you can use what you learned today?" Or, "How do you think we as a congregation can use what we learned?" (This last question will fit some chapters and not others.) Again, ask for short responses.

If you still have time left, you can ask: "What questions or concerns have been raised for you that you hope will be addressed in future sessions?" Listen to those responses and then encourage the group to keep them in mind while they read the next chapter. If you are working with a team, one team member can write down these questions so you can work some of them into future sessions.

Close with an announcement about what you will do next week—name the chapter to be discussed and any logistical information they may need to know (room change, the need to be here by 9:30 promptly because you will begin then). Thank the group for their participation and tell them you look forward to seeing them next week. If it is your tradition and you want to, you can close with a prayer, although usually the end of the group gets a bit noisy and ragged, with some people slipping out, children coming in, or others talking in the hallways. For this reason, we suggest beginning with prayer and ending on a practical note!

∽ Suggested 2-Hour Afternoon or Evening Session
Materials Needed
- A copy of the book being discussed for each participant
- A Bible for each participant
- A copy of *The Book of Common Prayer* and, if using music, *The Hymnal 1982* or other music
- An easel with newsprint, markers, and masking tape for the leaders
- Newsprint, markers, and masking tape for each small group
- A room where chairs can be arranged in a circle or semicircle
- Refreshments
- Music and a CD or cassette player (optional)
- VCR and TV (optional)
- Materials for a specific activity

Gathering Time:
10-15 minutes (before the announced session time)
Set up refreshments and the room so everything is ready at least 15 minutes before the announced session time. Hospitality is important—make sure the

table is inviting and that people are welcomed as they arrive. If you like, you can add fresh flowers to the table and/or soft music in the background as people gather. Provide name tags if the group is large or the group members do not know each other, especially if you opened the group to the community.

Starting the Session:
10 minutes
Introductions (first session)
Introduce the leaders and invite each participant to say their name, who they are, and what they hope to gain from the class. If the group is larger than eight or ten, one option is to do this in several small groups rather than one large one. You may need to adjust your times for the first session to include the introductions. Since they help the group to bond, it is best to cut a bit elsewhere and give people time to get to know each other and to articulate their hopes and fears.

Meditation
Select an appropriate scripture passage. Invite the group to reflect on the passage using the methods outlined in *Engaging the Word* or one of the methods from *In Dialogue With Scripture* or *The Doubleday Pocket Bible Guide.*[1] Alternatively, you can read the passage, offer a brief (five sentences or so) reflection on it, and invite people to reflect on it in silence for several minutes before asking them to offer any thoughts they have in response to the passage.

An opening prayer
Resist the temptation to merely rattle through a collect from the prayer book. This is an opportunity to model praying (versus reading a prayer). The tradi-

tional Episcopal greeting and response—"The Lord be with you," "And also with you"—is very useful in letting everyone know what is going to happen. But then pause for several seconds to allow yourself and others to become aware of God's presence. When you feel ready, _pray_ the collect you have selected or offer a prayer of your own. The reason you are starting with prayer is to ask God to be active in the session and to help people become aware that God is an active participant. So this is not just a formality—it is a means of being present to God, a way of attending to God's place and role in our lives.

Introducing the Session:
20 minutes

Invite participants to join with you in summarizing the chapter by listing the key points the author made in the chapter. Write each point on newsprint as it is mentioned and comment briefly on that point (a sentence or two). Have your own list prepared in advance so you can add any points they miss. A team works best here so that one person can write and another call on participants and comment on the items as they are being written. Either team member can add a comment about his or her reaction to the point being named.

Alternatively, design another way to introduce the chapter—a role-play, a panel discussion, a debate. (See the suggestions in Starting a Session in chapter three.)

In your introduction cover the main points the author makes and include comments about your own reaction to the text. Look at the questions the group will be discussing for ideas about which points are most likely to engender conversation. Do not answer the question for the group, but share your own thoughts and feelings. For example: "The author pres-

ents idea X, which I found a totally new way of looking at this. I had always assumed Y, but I am now
rethinking how I look at this question."

When you have finished the summary of the chapter, invite people is to voice the questions and concerns
that the chapter raised for them. Again, do not answer
the questions, just raise them and encourage others
who might also have questions to raise them in the
group discussion.

Discussing the Chapter:
30 minutes (includes about 5 minutes "travel
time" to the small groups)
Whether you have one group or several, now is the
time to begin the discussion questions. Each group
leader can direct the participants to the questions at
the end of the chapter (plus any others your group
may have generated and distributed) and invite discussion. Suggest they start with the question that
they are most attracted to, disturbed by, or energized
by rather than just taking them in order. Tell them
that after they have spent 5 to 10 minutes on that
question, they can select another question on the list
and proceed with discussing that one.

The main job of the group leader is to keep the discussion going and make sure all are included, using
the different techniques for guiding discussion found
in chapter three.

Break:
15 minutes
Encourage people to help themselves to refreshments,
visit the restrooms (make sure community members
unfamiliar with your church know where to find
them), and chat.

Make sure you resume promptly at the announced time, even if there are stragglers. If you start later, the group will know that you do not really intend to start in 15 minutes, so most of them will be even later the next week.

Reflection and Integration:
30 minutes

This time can be used for reflection and/or work on the activity suggested in this guide or an activity you develop. The purpose of this time is to give participants a chance to integrate what they have learned into their lives. (See chapters three and five for things to think about in planning and leading an activity.)

Reflection can be done alone or after an activity. If you are doing the reflection after an activity, you will need to shorten it to about 5 minutes. Ask questions that invite participants to name what they have learned and how they will use it. Ask: "What questions or concerns have been raised for you?" Write them on newsprint. If you are working with a team, one team member can write the first question or concern on one sheet of newsprint while the other team member writes the next one on a second sheet of paper. Work quickly to make a list. Then invite the group to look at the questions and concerns and select a couple to discuss. Ask: "Are there any questions here we think we can answer?" "Are there any concerns we would like to address?" Identify questions that will be addressed in later chapters and encourage the group to watch for them as they read the next chapter(s).

After about 10 minutes, ask participants: "What did you learn today?" "What was most important, exciting, or new to you?" You might want to give people a couple of minutes to jot down their thoughts before they share them. This allows people enough time to think and gives each participant a record of what they have learned. Encourage them to keep their list.

If or when the energy flags, ask: "How do you think you can use what you learned today?" Or, "How do you think we as a congregation can use what we learned?" (This last question will fit some chapters and not others.)

Close with an announcement about what you will do next week—name the chapter to be discussed and any logistical information the group needs to know (room change, the need to be here by 9:30 promptly because you will begin then). Thank the group for their participation and tell them you look forward to seeing them next week. Tell them you will close with worship and ask that participants leave quietly afterward. Invite anyone who wants to help you clean up the room after the service.

Closure:
10 minutes

If it is evening, we encourage you to use Compline (BCP 127) as a closing service. After several sessions, you may want to invite participants to lead the service. It is best to invite a specific person to do so at least a week ahead of time rather than asking for volunteers at the last minute. If your session is in the afternoon, you might want to use Evening Prayer (BCP 61 or 115) or An Order of Worship for the Evening (BCP 109). You can also use daily devotions for In the Early Evening (BCP 139) or At the Close of Day (BCP 140).

Whatever form of worship you use to close the session, try to avoid simply reading it in a hurried and harried fashion. Decide on how you will "set the stage" in a way that will enable the group to move into a prayerful space. You might, for example, pass out the prayer books while the worship leader clears your papers off the table at the front of the room (or, if you have not used one, brings out a small table). Set the table with a candle or two, perhaps the fresh flowers from the refreshment table, a copy of the book you are studying, and/or an icon. You might want to include a small amount of incense in a bowl.

When the books are distributed and people have found the page, invite them to sit in silence, being mindful of God's presence in your midst. Light the candles and incense. Sit in silence. Or put on music— a Taizé song, monastic chant, or other quiet gathering music. Practice beforehand so you can smoothly turn on and off the music lest the mechanics become overly distracting. When the leader is ready, begin the service.

When the service is finished, resist the temptation to shift abruptly into work mode. Speak in a softer tone, walk gently, and gradually move into cleaning up the room. This helps prevent the tendency to make worship a perfunctory thing we do and helps make it a prayerful experience.

∿ Retreats

While any of the books can be used as the basis of a retreat, several are more likely to fit this context. Before you select a book, consider the audience, purpose, and timing.

- Who will attend?
- Why are you doing the retreat and what do you plan to accomplish?
- When will the event take place? How long will it last?

Generally, we think of retreats as being more geared toward prayer and reflection than learning or discussing information. Retreats tend to be one day (usually Saturday), Friday night and Saturday, or perhaps all weekend. Occasionally they are as long as a week. But most congregations will be limited to one day up to the weekend.

Retreats can be built around several books. *The Practice of Prayer, Engaging the Word, Christian Wholeness*, and *Mysteries of Faith* are four that seem especially appropriate. One option is to invite the author to be the retreat leader, but if that is not possible, find someone who is a good retreat leader and identify ways to use the book. Again, the leader may use one or several chapters as "jumping off points" for a retreat talk and participants can read that chapter during the intervening quiet times. Or, if they read the book prior to the retreat, they can reflect on the questions in the book or do activities suggested by the retreat leader. A retreat can, of course, include small group discussion, but it is important to build in quiet time when people can be alone to pray or reflect on what they have heard or read.

A retreat day is often divided into several sessions—perhaps two in the morning and two or three in the afternoon. Each session can start and end with a brief worship service—a hymn or song, a passage of scripture or a psalm, and a prayer. A meditation, usually on the theme for the day, is given. The meditation can be given by a person or it can be a reading from a book or even a recorded reading or videotape (although the latter is often less effective).

After the meditation, people are invited to pray or reflect in silence. If possible, suggest places in the church or on the grounds outside where they can wander. And provide a list of suggestions so they know what to do—this is especially important if your group is not familiar with retreat days. Tell people where they can go. Explain that some may choose to sit and think. Others may want to pray. Still others may want to read (provide appropriate books). Some may even want to respond artistically (provide art supplies) or physically (provide maps of the area so people can walk without getting lost and set aside spaces where dancers can express themselves without disturbing others). If possible, create small meditative spaces with floor carpets or seats, candles, an altar, perhaps an icon, cross, or other object of reflection. You may also want to give participants suggestions for ways of praying from *The Practice of Prayer* or use some of the prayer activities outlined for that book in chapter five below.

In all of these cases, emphasize that each person needs to find a way to be silent before God. The way itself is not so important. The only rules are to observe silence and to respect the needs of others. Remind people when you will gather again and, if possible, ring a bell about 2 minutes before the start of the next session.

These retreat days often have meals taken in silence. Since this is a concept foreign to most people, it is best to provide a brief explanation. The reason for the silence is to enable us to focus on ourselves and our relationship with God and God's creation. Invite people to become aware of the food they are eating and the way God nourishes them physically and spiritually. Encourage them to become aware of how we communicate when words are not present. Ask them to reflect on why they think they feel either comfortable or uncomfortable with the silence. Invite them to learn from the experience.

Sometimes a book is read at the meal. If so, it is best to have everyone get their food and sit or stand waiting until all are served. Then have someone say grace and invite people to begin eating. While they are eating, a reader begins reading. Ask people to listen in silence when they have finished their meal. Read until all have finished eating. Then, close with a prayer and ask participants to return to the meeting room in silence.

If you have never organized a retreat before, it would be helpful to find an experienced retreat leader to discuss the logistics. The first question to ask is: Where will you hold the retreat? You can do it at your own church but it is often helpful to be in a less familiar place. Ask if you can use a neighboring church—especially if you know of one that has a quiet, prayerful worship space, a variety of small group/private sit-and-read spaces, and attractive grounds. See if there is a nearby monastery or convent—they are often available for retreats. A church conference center is another good choice. Ask your diocese for help in finding an appropriate site. Just make sure to find a place that is quiet and that has no other groups scheduled to be in the building that day, unless they are willing to observe the silence. Nothing is worse than trying to sit in silence while the voices and laughter of others wafts through the air, doors slam, the shouts of the youth group come in and out, or the vacuum cleaner roars as the sexton cleans a nearby room.

Identify the rooms you will need. At a minimum you will need one large meeting space—usually the sanctuary, chapel, or other room where you can create sacred space—and as many small rooms as you can get. The smaller rooms or private spaces need to have comfortable seating and quiet—classrooms on a hallway where the day care center is in operation is not conducive to quiet reflection! Discuss your needs with those in charge of the building. Often you can create appropriate spaces simply by temporarily rearranging the furniture to create private seating spaces.

And it would be helpful to include a space with books that people can buy or borrow. Of course, if you plan to include small group discussion, you need to identify rooms and arrange the chairs in them into a circle. You will also need a small group leader for each group.

Set up one space where people can find refreshments (clarify whether you or the facility will pay for these). If the facility allows, there can also be a designated "talking" space where those who find 30 to 60 minutes of silence difficult to maintain. If talking in this space will disturb the other participants, lean toward shorter quiet times and ring a bell or otherwise signal when it is okay for participants to talk. If your group is not accustomed to silence, it is best to post several signs around the facility inviting them to respect others' need for silence and directing people to designated "talking" spaces. One of the leaders may need to prowl the hallways to help people follow these norms, as a couple of people are likely to start a vigorous conversation while others nearby will be disturbed by it but are often unwilling to say anything. If possible, provide daycare for children in an area where joyful shrieks are distant enough to avoid distracting participants.

Retreats generally have very simple meals—soup, bread and cheese, salad, or sandwiches. If you are at a retreat center, they will generally provide meals. If not, consider having someone cater the meals. If the group will be cooking their own meals it is even more important to keep it simple—the idea is to be on retreat, not spend the day cooking, with only a few minutes to dash for the presentation. Spaghetti, bread, and a salad make a quick and easy dinner that almost everyone can help prepare.

If you have participants under the age of eighteen, obtain a signed consent form from their parents or guardians. Read *Better Safe than Sued*[2] or a comparable book for sample forms and things to consider when planning an event with youth—although most of it applies to any age group!

Make sure you have a contract with the facility you are using that spells out all the costs, rules, and expectations. This is especially important if it is an overnight retreat. Before the retreat inform all participants of emergency phone numbers, which they should leave with someone back home in case they need to be contacted during the event. When they arrive, inform them about emergency procedures—fire exits, location of fire extinguishers and first aid kits, and so on.

If the cost of the event is to be covered by the participants, add up the travel, food, and accommodation expenses and remember to include all of the "hidden costs"—pens, pencils, paper, books, snacks, flowers on the refreshment table, and so on. It is best to increase the charge enough to cover the inevitable unexpected expenses and, if appropriate, provide scholarship funds for those who might not otherwise be able to attend. If you should be fortunate enough to have a bit left over, save it for the next retreat. That's better than coming up short!

Suggested Weekend Retreat Format
Friday evening
    4:30   Arrivals begin—welcome and room/ facility familiarization
    5:30   Gathering time (refreshments and a place for people to meet each other)
    6:00   Welcome and an overview of the "norms" (meals, service times, and habits of a

religious order if you are meeting at their facility, schedule, and so on)

6:30   Dinner (if facility requires a 6 P.M. meal-time, shorten the welcome and do the rest later)

7:30   Opening worship, such as An Order of Worship for the Evening (BCP 109)

8:00   Meditation, perhaps on the retreat topic

8:30   Reading and reflection—time to read a suggested chapter and/or reflect on the meditation, journaling

9:30   Compline

Saturday

7:00   Morning Prayer or Matins (if worship-ing with a monastic community)

7:30   Breakfast

8:30   First session—talk on one of the chapters or a related topic

9:00   Reflection Time—silence, suggested read-ing and/or writing

10:00   Second session—talk on one of the chap-ters or a related topic

10:30   Reflection Time—silence, suggested read-ing and/or writing

11:30   Noonday prayers

12:00   Lunch

1:00   Free time

2:00   Third session—talk on one of the chap-ters or a related topic

2:30   Reflection time—silence, suggested read-ing and/or writing

3:30   Fourth session—talk on one of the chap-ters or a related topic

4:00   Reflection time—silence, suggested read-ing and/or writing

5:00   Evening worship
5:30   Fellowship time—refreshments
6:00   Dinner
8:00   Meditation
8:30   Reflection or discussion time
9:30   Compline

Sunday
7:00   Morning Prayer or Matins
7:30   Breakfast
8:30   Fifth session—talk on one of the chapters or a related topic
9:00   Reflection time—silence, suggested reading and/or writing
10:00 Sixth session—summary of retreat
10:30 Reflection time—silence, suggested reading and/or writing
11:30 Noonday prayers
12:00 Lunch and departures

⁓ **Conferences**

As with retreats, any of the books can be used as the basis of a conference, but some work better than others. Before you select a book, consider the audience, purpose, and timing.

• Who will attend?
• Why are you doing the conference and what do you plan to accomplish?
• When will the event take place? How long will it last?

Conferences tend to be more directed toward information and action than retreats: the purpose is to tell people about a topic in order to inspire them or give them the tools to act. Like retreats they tend to be either one day (usually Saturday) or Friday night and Saturday or perhaps all weekend. Occasionally they are as long as a week. But most congregations will be limited to one day up to the weekend.

Conferences could easily be built around *Christian Social Witness, Ethics After Easter, Living With History, Horizons of Mission,* and *The Anglican Vision,* either by having a series of speakers make presentations on each chapter and then have the group discuss them, or by asking people to read the book in preparation for the conference. Use the questions and activities suggested as a way to engage people in the topic.

Conferences often have several things going on at once, so you might have an opening keynote address by the author or someone with expertise in the topic and then give participants the choice of attending several workshops. If you are using one of the books, you might create a workshop that corresponds to each chapter in the book. Participants most likely would only go to workshops addressing two or three chapters, which then gives you an excellent opportunity to recommend the related book as a follow-up. Include a copy of this guide as part of their packet and encourage them to form a study group at home and incorporate what they learned at the conference. People are more likely to remember what they learned and act on it if they have some concrete immediate action that requires them to use what they learned at the conference.

Suggested Conference Format
One-Day Conference
Saturday

7:30	Breakfast
9:00	Opening session—welcome, announcements, opening worship

9:30   Keynote address (author, expert, or other
        motivational speaker who can address
        the topic)
10:30   Break
10:45   Questions and answers with the speaker
11:30   Noonday prayers
12:00   Lunch
1:30   First set of workshops (choose from x
        number available)
3:00   Break
3:30   Second set of workshops (choose from x
        number available)
5:00   Closure—thank yous, farewell, closing
        worship
5:30   Home

Friday evening/Saturday conference
Friday evening
5:30   Gathering time with refreshments
6:30   Dinner (or 6:00 with welcome at end of
        gathering time or after dinner)
8:00   Speaker
9:00   Compline or closing prayer
9:30   Fellowship

Saturday
7:30   Breakfast
9:00   Opening session—welcome to new
        arrivals, announcements, opening wor-
        ship
9:30   First set of workshops (choose from x
        number available; one might be with
        speaker)
10:30   Break
10:45   Finish first workshop
12:00   Lunch

1:30 Second set of workshops (choose from x number available)
3:00 Break
3:30 Third set of workshops (choose from x number available)
5:00 Closure—thank yous, farewell, closing worship
5:30 Home

Chapter Five

Suggested Activities for Each Volume

~ Activities for *The Anglican Vision*

Denomination and Faith Comparison Chart

Invite the participants in the group to create a comparison chart of various denominations and faith groups (Roman Catholic, Lutheran, Jewish, Muslim) they have belonged to or are interested in. It is probably best not to get into too many groups lest this become an extensive research project. The purpose of this activity is to help participants gain a clearer sense of what is unique about Anglicanism.

Find a large wall space—perhaps a hallway or six-foot or longer wall—preferably in or near your meeting room. Cover the wall with newsprint. (You can ask your local newspaper if you can purchase a roll of newsprint.) Be sure to put up *two* layers of newsprint so the markers you use will not mar the walls.

Down the left side of the newsprint, write the names of the denominations and faith groups you will be comparing. Leave one blank space at the top for the topic headings and a couple at the bottom for later additions. Draw a horizontal line under each denomination and carry it across the entire length of the paper. Then, draw a few vertical columns—just enough to get you started. You will add others later. In the vertical columns, pick headers that parallel the chapters. Your newsprint should look something like this:

	1 HISTORY/ ORIGINS	2 TRADITION/ CHANGE	3 THEOLOGY	4 MISSION	5 CORE BELIEFS	6 WORSHIP	7 AUTHORITY	8 SACRAMENTS
EPISCOPAL								
METHODIST								
PRESBYTERIAN								
CONGREGATIONAL								
ROMAN CATHOLIC								
SOUTHERN BAPTIST								
LUTHERAN								
PENTECOSTAL								
JEWISH								
MUSLIM								

During the registration process, and before the first meeting, invite participants to gather around the chart and fill in the first column. Remind them to write small! Ask them to sign their names next to the denominations they have experience or knowledge of and to indicate by code their level of experience or knowledge. Do this by printing the following legend below the chart:

1 = childhood experience: went to church and Sunday school but don't remember much

2 = childhood knowledge: studied and remember some of it

3 = youth experience: went to church and/or youth group

4 = youth knowledge: attended confirmation classes or equivalent

5 = adult experience: just attended church, did not study much

6 = adult knowledge: attended inquirers' class, took a class in college, other study.

Some people will have just one number; others may have several. In any case, it will give you a picture of the group's experience. As you can tell from this, you will want to write the denomination names at the top of the box so there is room for group members to write below. Again, write small. And make the Episcopal row larger than the rest.

After each session, gather around the newsprint and fill in the chapter spaces. Those who have experience and knowledge of a denomination can take the lead in filling in those spaces. In some cases, you will need to encourage the group members to interview someone from another denomination or to do some research to fill in the blanks.

If the chart is constructed in the meeting space, move it out into public space after the last session and invite the congregation to review the chart. This is a good way to encourage others to join the group should you choose to offer it again. And it will give others at least a glimpse at the differences between various denominations and faith groups.

It is likely that the group members will ask for the chart to be typed up and distributed—especially if they have put much work into it. Arrange to do this and keep it on file. If you do additional groups, you can add the wisdom of one group to the next and, over time, build up a fairly comprehensive comparison chart.

Denomination and Faith Group Visits
This activity is designed to be a continuation of the group studying *The Anglican Vision*. After the group has read and discussed the book, arrange for them to attend the services of several other denominations (Sunday morning, evening and/or weekday services).

Before the visits, take one session for the group to discuss what they will look for. Use the categories listed on the comparison chart above as a starting point. Obviously, they will look for differences in worship styles. But they can also observe differences in authority (beliefs about the scriptures, the names of key leaders, and so on), theology, mission, or tradition.

Develop a list of questions or categories to remind participants of focal areas as they reflect on their experience. They will need to separate their experience of a particular congregation from the experience of the whole denomination's worship, theology, and tradition. Encourage them to attend the service with at least one other person and to take time immediately after the service to take notes—but not during the service or in the church.

It is best if the visitors come early and plan to stay for any education program and/or coffee hour. Ask them to gather available documents—a bulletin, other handouts, visitors' cards, or brochures. Remind them to look at the bulletin boards and walls for signs and symbols that give them clues to this denomination's beliefs and practices. If there is a library or book display, see what is available.

Tell the clergy of the church you are visiting who you are and why you are attending their service. You can do this by letter in advance, indicating that you do not expect or want any special attention, merely that you are informing him or her of your presence as a courtesy. Or you can mention it when greeting the clergy on the day of your visit.

The focus of the visit is to ask: "What is *different* from what I experience in the Episcopal Church?" This is not an evaluative question—a question that attempts to decide if the observed difference is good or bad. Rather, it is descriptive. *What* is different? Encourage group members to merely describe what differences they experienced or observed without trying to make sense of the differences.

The group can meet as usual either between visits or after two visits. When the group gathers, invite each team to report on their observations. This will probably take at least one or two sessions (depending on the size of the group). Once all the initial reports have been given, invite the group to reflect on the differences and talk about why the other churches did things differently or expressed beliefs that were different from ours. This is the point where the group tries to make sense of what they saw and experienced. It becomes important here to separate the experience of a particular group of people from the denomination. In other words, did we find Church X especially welcoming or prayerful because it was the ethos of that particular congregation, or because these characteristics are inherent in the denomination's practices and beliefs?

Help the members of the group focus on each of the denominations in turn. Remember that the goal is to understand the differences, not to either glorify or denigrate the Episcopal Church. Understanding the differences will help people value what we have without labeling what others have as "better" or "worse." If you find the comparisons taking on a critical tone, remind the participants of the group's goal to understand denominations other than our own.

∽ Activities for *Opening the Bible*

Gospel Reading

Opening the Bible has activities included in the chapter questions. For example, it asks group members to read the gospel of Mark as part of preparing for the discussion of the third chapter. Reading the gospel of Mark aloud is something a number of people, including prominent actors, have done as powerful performance pieces, and you can also obtain a video of a professional reading the gospel of Mark.[1] Schedule the video or audiotape at a time when other members of the congregation can participate. And remember to advertise it in your local newspaper, inviting members of the community to come. You can plan a lunch after church followed by the video/audiotape, or you can use it as an evening activity with small group discussion afterward, complete with coffee, tea, and dessert.

If you have an excellent reader or actor/actress in your congregation or community, you might also plan a live reading. This is actually more powerful *if* the person is able to read well enough to hold people's interest. If you choose to do this, think about the ambiance and establish a setting that will heighten the impact of the experience. For example, you might want to have all the lights in the room off except a single spotlight shining down on the reader who is dressed in black, sitting on a stool and reading from an adjustable book stand. If you keep the setting "normal" with all the lights on and all the usual distractions of sight and sound, it will be hard for people to listen attentively.

Create a sense of drama but do not overly dramatize the text. In other words, this is a reading, not a reenactment. You want people actually to hear the story. Remember, most people have never heard the story of Jesus in one sitting, so this could be a powerful experience for them.

Think about how you will open and close the session. You can, for example, simply begin with a brief welcome and then ask people to settle into a few minutes of silence. Turn off the lights. Have the reader come forward and kneel before the clergyperson, who then blesses the reader before he or she begins. At the end, the reader can simply close the Bible, stand, hold the Bible before the people (as in a gospel procession), and proclaim: "The Gospel of the Lord," to which people will give the normal response, "Praise to you, Lord Christ." Or the reader can silently place the Bible on the altar and leave with the group, maintaining a moment of silence before the leader closes with a prayer (the collect for Proper 28 on page 236 of *The Book of Common Prayer* would be appropriate).

If you are going to do small group discussion during the same evening, adjourn to another room. Since it will take about 90 minutes to read the gospel, you may want to schedule the discussion for the following Sunday morning. If you have done this as part of your ongoing group, you can invite all attendees to the discussion and simply divide them into two or more smaller groups, with your original study group in a group by themselves. Obviously, you will need to recruit additional small group leaders—preferably not your leadership team or original study group. If you do this before the study group begins, you can use it as a way to invite people into the group.

During the discussion, ask people to talk about how the experience affected them. Ask: "How did you react to the reading? What were you thinking and feeling as you listened? What impact did it have on you in the next day or two? What did you learn about Jesus? What did you learn about yourself? What did you learn about the scriptures? What, if anything, did you feel led to be or do as a result of the reading?"

∿ Activities for *Engaging the Word*
Ways to Study the Bible
Engaging the Word describes several ways of studying the Bible in chapter four, including the African Bible Study method. *In Dialogue With Scripture* and *The Doubleday Pocket Bible Guide*[2] Both have a dozen additional methods—each of which is outlined in a few simple steps. Try several of the methods and discuss what each of them offers to individuals or to groups.

Encourage the group to try these methods at home with family members or friends and report on their experience. Point out several that engage the senses (artistic or writing) or that are geared toward children (crazy questions). Invite the group to discuss their experience and describe what leading a group was like for them. Many people think that they need to be biblical experts or at least relatively knowledgeable about the Bible in order to lead Bible study. These methods do not assume such expertise. They invite the group to learn together.

Biblical Storytelling

Set aside a session or an afternoon, perhaps after church on Sunday, to do biblical storytelling. The National Association of Biblical Storytellers has a network of folks, both professional and volunteer, who are available to do workshops.[3] They also have a video that demonstrates biblical storytelling. This is an activity that can involve all ages

Take a story passage from the Bible—choose something that is reasonably short and yet interesting. Invite group members to take turns reading it. The first time, suggest reading the passage in a normal tone of voice. The second time, emphasize the nouns; the third time, the verbs. Then have someone else read it slowly, sentence by sentence, while the rest of the group imagines the scene. Invite the group to get up and move in response to the story—point, gesture, look in the direction the speaker would look, and so on. Then have them repeat the story from memory, line by line, using gestures as they go. Biblical storytelling incorporates body movement, voice, and text so you need to gradually encourage people to use all of themselves in telling the story. Finally, have the participants tell the story to each other in small teams of two or three.

After you have learned and told a story, take some time to talk about the experience. What did you learn about the passage? What was different for you this time? What did you learn about yourself?

～ Activities for *The Practice of Prayer*
Quiet Day/Retreat

At the end of your study group, schedule a quiet day/retreat for the group members and the congregation (and local community). You can invite a leader from outside the congregation to lead this retreat or have the clergyperson or a skilled lay person from your congregation serve as leader. Another way to do this is for the group itself to plan and lead the retreat. If you are not experienced with retreats, invite your clergyperson or an experienced person to help you plan. (See the suggestions for planning a retreat in chapter four above.)

Additional Prayer Methods

The following three prayer methods can be tried at home during the week, incorporated into a retreat day, or practiced during a session. If you do any of these in the group, it might be helpful to adjourn to the sanctuary or a chapel and to alert others in the area to the need for silence.

Take some time to introduce these ways and discuss them. Many people are not familiar with these ways of praying and may find them uncomfortable at first. Remind participants that there is no right or wrong way to pray, and encourage them simply to try a method without judgment and then decide if it works for them. Explain that people are often surprised by what does work for them; it may have more to do with the core essence of who we are and where we are on our spiritual journey than with our prior spiritual experience.

Praying with a Picture or Icon

Read the following steps a couple of times and then begin:

1) Select a picture or painted icon of Jesus, the Trinity, Mary, or a saint. Place it in a position where you can view it without obstruction and find a comfortable position for yourself close to the picture.

2) Close your eyes and express, in words or without, your desire to experience God's presence through the picture and your desire to give up whatever might prevent or block that experience. If you are using a picture of Jesus, you might silently repeat his name in rhythm with your breathing.

3) When you feel centered, open your eyes and look at the picture. Look into the eyes and spend a moment reaching for God through the eyes of the icon. Let go of any thoughts that emerge (imagine them floating away from the picture in bubbles). Keep your eyes very still and just focus on letting yourself be known to God through the icon's eyes. Remain in that place of God seeing and knowing you for about 15 to 20 minutes, or until you feel ready to move on.

4) When you are ready, close your eyes and mentally envision the picture. Let it slowly fade as you gradually become the icon. Then try to sense the eyes of the icon reappearing as *your* eyes, God seeing the world through you. In your imagination, look out from the icon with the eyes of God and see what emerges. Rest in this for a moment and then gradually return to the room by becoming aware of your body, what is around you, and then opening your eyes.

When you are finished, reflect on the following questions: What was it like to let yourself be seen and known by God? What did you feel? What happened when the eyes of the icon became your eyes? Was there any moment when you especially felt God's presence?

Praying with an Object
Read the following steps a couple of times and then begin:

1) Select an object as the focal point for your prayer. This might be a nature object, like a stone, or a sacred object, like a cross. Place it near you or position yourself where you can easily reach out and touch it.

2) Close your eyes and express, in words or without, your desire to experience God's presence through the object, and your desire to give up whatever might prevent or block that experience.

3) When you feel centered, open your eyes and look at the object for awhile.

4) Then close your eyes and touch the object, turn it over in your hands, feel its texture, smell it. If it makes a sound, listen to it—perhaps even taste it. Do this slowly, with your eyes closed. Use each of your senses to explore the object.

5) Now open your eyes and look at it again, this time from different angles. Turn it around and over; examine it closely without giving a thought to anything else.

6) When you have thoroughly explored your object, think about its functions. What is its place in the world? Give thanks to God for creating this object and the world.

7) Then consider possible symbolic associations. What things in your life come to mind as you reflect on this object? Pray that God will reveal what you can learn from it but do not worry about whether you get any big revelations or not. Just ask the question.

8) Ask whether the object suggests a course of action. Sometimes it will, sometimes it will not.

9) Talk with God about what you have felt, discovered, or learned.

When you have finished, reflect on these questions: What did you feel, discover, or learn about yourself, the object, and God? Did your meditation take you into a different way of being with God?

Praying the Rosary

To pray the entire Rosary you begin at the crucifix with the Apostles' Creed, then say the Lord's Prayer (1st bead), three Hail Mary's (next 3 beads), and a *Gloria Patri* (last single bead). You then go around the entire circle of beads three times (once for each set of mysteries listed below), repeating Hail Mary's on each of the ten beads and the Lord's Prayer on the single beads. However, you may want to begin with just one of the mysteries, either the joyful (especially in Advent) or sorrowful (especially in Lent). You can also use the Nativity, Agony in the Garden, Crucifixion, Resurrection, and Descent of the Holy Spirit. Also, if you do not want to use the Hail Mary prayer, you can use another prayer, such as the *Sanctus*, the Jesus Prayer, or John 3:16, instead.

Once you are ready to begin your selected mystery, pause for a moment before each decade (set of ten beads) to read and recall the event it symbolizes. Then begin saying the Hail Mary's while simultaneously meditating on the event. This will feel rather awkward, like rubbing your stomach and patting your head at the same time! But hang in there. Eventually the recitation of the prayers will fall into the background and you can focus on the event. The prayers will become automatic and will occupy that part of your mind that wants to think about something else and distract you from focusing on the event. Sometimes it helps to envision a picture of the event and hold that in your mind. Go slowly, breathe deeply, and relax into the prayer space.

The Joyful Mysteries:
• The Annunciation of Jesus' birth to Mary by the angel Gabriel
• The Visitation of Mary to Elizabeth before John the Baptist's birth
• The Nativity (birth of the Christ child)
• The Presentation of Jesus in the temple
• Finding Jesus in the temple amazing the elders with his wisdom

The Sorrowful Mysteries:
• Agony in the Garden of Gethsemane
• Scourging at the pillar during the trial
• Crowning of Jesus with the crown of thorns
• Jesus carrying his cross to Golgotha
• Crucifixion of Jesus

The Glorious Mysteries:
• Resurrection of Jesus
• Ascension of Jesus
• Descent of the Holy Spirit at Pentecost
• Assumption of Mary into heaven
• Coronation of Mary as Queen of Heaven

The Hail Mary prayer said at each bead is:

Hail, Mary, full of grace, the Lord is with you; blessed are you among women, and blessed is the fruit of your womb, Jesus. Holy Mary,

Mother of God, pray for us sinners, now and at the hour of our death. Amen.

The *Gloria Patri* is:

Glory to the Father, and to the Son, and to the Holy Spirit; as it was in the beginning, is now, and will be for ever. Amen.

～ Activities for *Living With History*
Congregational Timeline

After studying chapter two in the book you can add a session during which you build a historical timeline for your congregation. This activity can be with the group alone or open to the rest of the congregation.

First, gather as much resource material about the congregation's history as may be available—written histories, archival documents, oral stories, and so on. Put sheets of newsprint along a large wall space—at least eight to ten feet long. (Remember to put double sheets so the markers will not bleed through and damage the walls.) Draw a horizontal line along the center of the paper and mark the decades between the founding of your congregation and the current date.

During the session, invite people to divide into roughly equal groups and take responsibility for several decades. If you are a relatively new church, each small group may only cover ten or twenty years. In an older church, each group may cover fifty years. Distribute the materials you gathered and invite the groups to write brief notes on vertical lines at the appropriate dates.

There are different date markers you might want to suggest—pick just one or two at the most or your timeline will get too messy to be useful! Or you can do several timelines, each with a different focus.

• Identify *significant events* and place them above the horizontal line. These might be dates when buildings were started or completed or new ministries were launched or ended; the date of the largest number of children in church school; the time when the building was flooded. Below the line, list *significant people* of the congregation. These might mark the comings and goings of each rector; the death of a founder or other significant members; the names of people from that congregation entering the priesthood or diaconate; the first election of a woman to the vestry.
• Identify *congregational events* above the line and *community/world events* below the line.
• Identify events that mark the congregation's *spiritual journey* above the line and events that mark its *temporal journey* below the line. In this case, events like initiating adult education, significant increases in new members or stewardship, and expanded lay ministry would go above the line, while church buildings and rectors coming and going would go below the line.
• Identify *changes in ministry* in your congregation. Who did which ministries? When did changes occur? Put congregational changes above the line and denominational, community, or world changes below the line. Use some of the touchstones in chapter two of the book: When was the civil rights movement and how did it affect the congregation? When did the Episcopal Church include women on vestries or ordain women, and how did those changes affect the congregation?

• Invite the entire congregation to write their names at the *date when they joined* this congregation. See what patterns emerge.

• Identify the *congregation's journey* above the line and the *diocese/national church's journey* below the line. (This one will require a fair amount of knowledge about the diocese and national church that may not be readily available.)

After you have constructed your timeline, invite the group to use it during the sessions that follow. As different topics are discussed, they may want to add additional information to the timeline. For example, they might add controversies in a different color marker after studying chapter four. Encourage them to reflect on those questions about the congregation's history: What does it tell us about ourselves? How has our history contributed to who we are? How can we work with parts of our history that still have an impact on us? How can we recycle our tradition(s)? How can we renew them?

～ Activities for *Early Christian Traditions*
Who is God? Who is Jesus?

Find two large open spaces on a wall in a public area in the church and post at least four sheets of newsprint in each space. Create a square (or a rectangle with six sheets) at a good height for reading and writing (low enough for children; high enough for tall folks). Remember to put a backing sheet behind each sheet so the markers do not damage your walls.

On one square write the header "Who is God?" and on the other write "Who is Jesus?" For a couple of Sundays prior to the group meeting and for the first week or two, encourage any one of any age to write their thoughts on the paper. They can use just a word or phrase, draw a picture, write a quotation, or whatever they think conveys who God and Jesus are. These contributions should be anonymous so people can feel free to say whatever they want. Make sure that children and youth are included. Provide lots of markers in different colors (water-based so they do not ruin clothes or walls). Make it fun.

After the group has discussed the book, invite participants to write their own answers to these questions. Then take some time to read and discuss the comments people wrote on the newsprint. Ask the group to identify any strains of heretical or orthodox teachings from other ages in the comments. If a comment sounds like a specific theologian or time period, mark it on the sheet. Talk about how people develop their understanding of who God and Jesus are and how the church can be involved in forming that understanding. When you have finished, invite participants to look at their own answers and say if or how their answers today might have changed since the course began. What is the value of looking at our tradition and what it says about these questions? What difference does it make?

Depending on how the discussion goes and especially on what your congregation has written, you might want to ask the group if they would like to engage others in the congregation in this discussion. For example, if your sheets reveal a high amount of unorthodox thinking, ask what they could do to help others in the congregation learn about the church's teaching on God and Jesus. You might develop a plan to address some of the beliefs that surfaced in the writing and discussion.

～ Activities for *Opening the Prayer Book*

Experience Worship in Other Traditions

Divide the group into small teams to visit other churches and experience their way of worshiping. You can do this one Sunday morning and then discuss how those worship experiences differ from the Episcopal liturgy. If you have already read some of the history and tradition books (*The Anglican Vision, Living With History, Early Christian Traditions, A Theology of Worship*), discuss why those differences are present. Identify elements in the service that are similar even if not quite the same. Where did they come from? Why did they survive all these centuries?

Experience Worship in Our Tradition

Ask the group to select one or more earlier versions of *The Book of Common Prayer* and then plan and lead a worship service as it would have been done at that time. Encourage them to do research, including interviews with older members of the congregation who might remember worshiping with that prayer book. Locate copies of sermons from that time. Find out how the furniture was arranged, what people wore, and how they interacted. Invite the entire congregation to participate—some may choose to come in period dress as well. Give the congregation information about what to expect ahead of time.

Afterward, serve refreshments and engage people in a discussion of what they experienced, how they responded, and what they learned from it. Invite them to explore what has changed in our liturgy and why. Describe when and where it would have been used, and engage people in looking at what has changed and why. What was happening in the church and world at the time? What changes were important to the American church?

⁓ **Activities for** *Mysteries of Faith*
Going Beyond Words

The reading and discussion in this book are more abstract than in some of the others. To balance that and help people integrate what they have been discussing, plan a creative session toward the end of the course. Invite people to come in casual clothes that will enable them to be creative and explain that the group will have an opportunity to explore the mysteries in art, writing, music, or dance.

Some people will be nervous about this idea, so assure them that this will be a time to meditate on one of the concepts and create something for themselves— they will not have to show it to anyone if they do not want to. Explain that there will be one creative room with quiet music and places for artists and writers to work and other spaces for music and dance folks. (If you do not have room, you can eliminate the music and dance options.) Ask each person to pick one of the mysteries to focus on next week—trinity, creation, revelation, incarnation, salvation, and eschatology. Assemble a wide variety of creative supplies:

• Art supplies such as paints, colored markers, crayons, chalk, scissors, rulers, magazines, string, glue, tidbits of various sorts (buttons, glitter, scraps of colored paper), clay, colored felt, fabrics, poster board, colored paper, newsprint, white paper, tissue paper

• Music supplies such as lined music paper, hymnals, piano music or other sheet music, instruments (you can invite people who play instruments to bring them)

• Dance supplies such as music sources (CD player with CDs), space for people to create, scarves or other supplies; invite people who

might want to create in this way to bring CDs
they like
• Writing supplies such as paper (various sizes
and types), pens, poetry books, computer (if
available)
Before people arrive, put on soft instrumental
music or chant to play in the background. As people
arrive, invite them to find a spot and create something
in response to the mystery they have. Ask people to
leave when they are finished, taking their artwork
with them, and meet for a final session the following
week. If they want to, they can bring their creation or
they can just reflect on the creative process.

During the last session, take about half of the
session for people to either talk about what they
experienced in the creative session and/or to show
what they did. Take the last half of the session for
people to reflect on what they learned from the
entire experience.

～ Activities for *Ethics After Easter*
Movies, Movies, Movies!
Rent a video that addresses one or more of the ethical
issues identified in this book. Watch the movie and
spend time identifying these questions. Do not try to
solve them, just identify them and discuss the factors
that contribute to them. What institutions in society
have a vested interest in the issue (for example, the
health care system, educational institutions, the
media, the judicial system)? One movie Holmgren discusses in the book is *The Fugitive*, in which a doctor on
the run gets into a hospital disguised as an orderly
and changes a child's treatment plan. Other possible
movies include: *The Apostle*, *The Cider House Rules*, *The
Insider*, *Erin Brockovich*, and *The Rainmaker*.

Examining Ethical Issues
Ask the group to name current ethical issues that they care about. List them on newsprint. Give each person two sticky dots or stars (for example, one red dot and one blue dot) and ask the group to put the red dots on their first choice and the blue dots on their second choice. Or use another method to narrow the list to enough issues to form small groups of about six people. Ask each group to use Holmgren's three-step method (described in chapter eight) to discuss their issue and see if they can build a moral case using that method. Give the groups one session to work together and a second session to report to each other. Encourage them to focus on learning the method rather than trying to "prove" any given position.

～ Activities for *Christian Social Witness*
Reaching Out to Others
The following activity helps people move from seeing those who are homeless, poor, elderly, or disabled as "them"—as people who are other than and less than we are—to recognizing that anyone could be in the same situation.[4] Learning to "love one another as Christ loved us" is much more difficult than just giving some "poor soul" a couple of hours of our time or a couple of dollars. Loving someone requires having a relationship with them that is more than just a one-time event in a one-up, one-down way of relating.

First choose an outreach activity to participate in as a group: for example, serving lunch at a local soup kitchen. In preparation for the event, invite the group to read the first two chapters of the book of Ruth. Ask: "How did Ruth and Naomi come to be homeless? What was their contribution to their situation—in other words, what did they do to cause their misfortune? How does this compare to homeless people today?

How does Boaz respond to Ruth's situation? What happens when he discovers that she is a relative? What would happen to those serving the poor if they discovered that a relative was among that day's guests? What does it mean to respond to the poor as if they were our brothers and sisters?"

Then read Genesis 18:1-8. Ask the group: "What does Abraham do for his unexpected guests? Who are Abraham's guests?" Remind them that they are the Lord or the angels of the Lord—Abraham entertains God and his angels without knowing it at the time. So too, those whom we serve can be, and are, the Christ in our midst.

After the Bible study, ask the group to role-play the situation they will be entering (in our example, going to serve a meal at a soup kitchen). The leaders and a couple of additional people can be the servers who will take on various roles of the "do-gooder," the person who looks down on the poor, the person who is over-ly solicitious. The rest of the group take on the roles of the homeless and hungry.

After the role-play ask: "What happened to you during this role-play? What contributed to that feeling? What would have made you feel empowered or loved? What contributes to people's feelings of disem-powerment? What would you want to have happen to you if, or when, you are hungry, poor, or homeless?" Make sure you talk about how they will apply what they learned from this experience to their service.

On the day of your outreach activity, meet as a group ahead of time. Answer any questions. Remind them of what you discussed in the preparation time and ask if there is anything they have thought of or learned since then that they would like to share before you go to the soup kitchen. Review any behavioral norms that may apply.

Before you begin your work, take time to pray. Invite the group to offer short prayers. After the meal or work period, gather for a time of reflection. It is best if you can do this either in the group's regular meeting room or in the sanctuary. Talk about what they experienced. Ask: "What was this experience like for you? What were you thinking and feeling? What did you learn about our guests? What did you learn about yourself? What might we do differently next time? What might we repeat? Did you experience God's presence? How? Did you see Christ in other members of the group and in the guests? How is Christian service different from service by a non-believer? How can we be Christ-bearers in our service? In our daily lives?"

∿ Activities for *Horizons of Mission*
Meeting Your Companion Diocese

If your diocese has a companion diocese in the southern hemisphere, such as in Africa or Latin America, take some time to explore the relationship.[5] If your congregation is unfamiliar with it, gather information about the diocese and the country where it is located and spend a session just learning about the life of Anglicans in another part of the world. Then use a second session to focus on what it means to be "partners." Ask: "How can people from two very different life circumstances be partners? How can you avoid the situation where the northern hemisphere diocese gives only of its material wealth and the southern hemisphere diocese gives only of its spiritual wealth? What else might both partners have to give? What else might they need to receive? Is partnership about giving and receiving at all?"

If you have the time and energy, you might want to engage in a long-distance dialogue by letter or email with members of a congregation from your companion diocese.

Reading the Bible with Third-World Eyes

Robert McAfee Brown's *Unexpected News: Reading the Bible with Third World Eyes* has a series of Bible studies that challenges northern hemisphere readers to look at the scriptures from the perspective of Christians living in the southern hemisphere.[6] Invite the group to try one of the exercises suggested in the book.

For example, print in four paragraphs the following passages: Exodus 1:8–14; 2:23–25; 3:7–8; 3:9–10. These four snippets capture the essence of the story in the fifteen chapters of Exodus, and are the theme of the whole Bible. Robert Brown identifies four main points:

1) A class struggle is going on.
2) God is aware of the struggle.
3) God takes sides in the struggle.
4) God calls people to join in the struggle.

Invite the group to read the passage and discuss each of these points. Encourage them to talk about how people in the southern hemisphere might hear this passage. Ask: "What is their life like? Who will they identify with? What parallels are they likely to draw to their situation? Who will they see as the oppressors? How are they likely to experience God in this passage? What are they likely to hear God's call to join in the struggle? How do you imagine they feel when they read and reflect on this story?" (If you have a companion diocese in the southern hemisphere, think about these questions from the perspective of people living in that diocese.)

Then ask: "How do we hear the Exodus story?" Go through each paragraph and each summary point.

Make sure the group does not avoid the hard realities by individualizing it—keep them focused on the northern hemisphere, that is, those who control the wealth and power in the world. It is all too easy to translate the story into our personal lives and see ourselves as the oppressed rather than face being part of the oppressor group. Keep encouraging them to think about how those in the southern hemisphere are likely to see the situation, given their circumstances. Encourage the group to talk about the dynamics between the haves and have nots and their discomfort about their position. Help the group understand that being born in the land of plenty means you are part of these dynamics simply because you live here—not because you do anything. Ask: "If God is on the side of the oppressed, how do we experience God? What do we hear in God's call to join the struggle? How do we feel about the Exodus story?"

Finally, ask the group: "How can we deal with the differences between these readings of the story? If we find ourselves on the wrong side of the struggle, can we change sides? If so, how? If God is on the side of the oppressed, what does it mean to be on God's side?"

∿ Activities for *A Theology of Worship*
Comparing Prayer Books from Various Cultures

One way to understand the various theologies that undergird our liturgies in the Episcopal Church is to get copies of as many of the historical versions of *The Book of Common Prayer* as you can, including the American prayer books of 1789 and 1928. The 1662 prayer book is still readily available and in use in England; also try to obtain copies of the current Canadian and New Zealand prayer books.

Look at them closely, particularly those services with which you are most familiar (the eucharist,

Morning Prayer, Evening Prayer, baptism). Photocopy or print sections from each in parallel so you can see exactly what changed from book to book. Track the changes in the liturgies on newsprint and record as many of the theological or cultural influences that affected them as you can find. Ask: "How have Anglican liturgies changed over time? How did cultural or political events shape our liturgies? What changes in theology can be discerned in these liturgical revisions?"

It might also be interesting to use selections from the various prayer books as part of your group life and/or incorporate them into the congregation's services. How do the prayers and rubrics differ from those in the American *Book of Common Prayer*? How are they similiar? What do these differences/similarities tell us about their theologies of worship? Members of the group may well have worshiped in Anglican churches while traveling abroad. Ask them to describe their experiences, and perhaps to lead parts of the services from those prayer books.

For example, *A New Zealand Prayer Book* has some beautiful prayers that can be used in a regular Sunday morning service. But it is also interesting to see how they have incorporated the native Maori people's language and culture into the book. It probably provides the best basis from which to discuss how culture and theology inform our worship. (Order early if you want to use the *New Zealand Prayer Book*. It has become so popular that it is often difficult to obtain.)

～ Activities for *Christian Wholeness*
Mission of the Church
The mission of the church as stated in the catechism (BCP 855) is focused on wholeness: "The mission of the church is to restore people to unity with God and

each other in Christ." Write this statement on newsprint and invite the group to discuss what it means to them. Ask: "How does the church restore people to unity with God? With each other? How is Christ involved in that?" Then say something like the following, in your own words:

> Any organization's mission is its primary purpose—the reason for its existence. In industry identifying the primary business is relatively easy: it is the product or service the company provides. In a church it is not quite so easy, but it is equally essential. The first thing we need to decide is, what business are we in? Some people think we are in the business of providing information about religion (in this case, Christianity). Some think we are in the business of providing charity—goods and services to the needy not provided by government or community agencies. Some think we are in the business of providing worship services. Some think we are in the business of teaching values. . . .
>
> The mission of the Episcopal Church as defined in the prayer book is "to restore people to unity with God and each other in Christ." That is our main business—our purpose for existing. All the activities and programs and services and resources we provide should help us do that primary business of reconciliation. So today we are going to look at our congregation's ministry and see how it matches this mission. . . .

Ask the group to describe the present ministry of your congregation by listing the ministry activities on sheets of newsprint. Then ask them to measure their current ministry against the mission statement of the church. Look at each ministry activity and ask whether this restores people to unity with God and each other in Christ.

• Use different color Post-It cards to post alongside each item, or use a different color marker to mark each item. You may want to mark them "Strong," "Weak," and "Not really" or "Only indirectly," or use whatever system you and the group find comfortable. The goal is to get a picture of how many of your activities actually help you do your main business of reconciliation.

• Ask the group to create a sentence: We do "x" (activity) to produce "y" (the end result) which restores people to God (and each other) in Christ. (Just do a few examples, not all of them!)

• Be firm and do not let the group justify everything as reconciliation. Ask: How does "x" activity restore people to unity? Is this a simple coming together, or is it unity "in Christ"? How would we recognize true reconciliation?

Ask, again and again, "What do we do that makes us different from all other organizations?" If we are no different from anyone else, we either do not know what business we are in or we are doing someone else's business! A laundromat and dry cleaner both are in the business of cleaning clothes, but you know which service you want for which clothes. A psychologist and a medical doctor may both be in the business of restoring people to health, but you can tell the difference between them. What we do, as Christians, needs to be clearly and distinctly *Christian*. Help people understand that while most church activities are good, some may not help us accomplish our mission.

If you identify those activities, talk about what purpose they do serve. And point out that if the organization's energy is devoted to many activities that are not mission-focused, the organization may not be able to accomplish its primary mission and thus may not really be "the church" but merely a "church-like entity."

The Rite of Reconciliation

If your congregation is not familiar with the Rite of Reconciliation, this might be a good time to introduce it. Begin by looking at the mission of the church on page 855 of *The Book of Common Prayer* (see outline above for ideas on how to introduce and discuss it). Then invite the participants to read the Rite of Reconciliation, stopping at each point to discuss what is happening and why. Encourage the group to talk about different ways in which individuals might want or need to come to reconciliation—for example, public or private confession. Talk about the four stages of reconciliation:

> *Confess my sin:* Recognize and acknowledge honestly before God and other Christians what I have done; feel the guilt and sorrow that comes with seeing the pain I have caused; accept responsibility for my actions.
>
> *Make amends:* Do whatever I can to "make it right" for those affected by my action: apologize, pay for therapy, or for pain and suffering; resign from a position of leadership; spend time in prison.
>
> *Seek amendment of life:* Do whatever is necessary to make sure that I do not repeat the behavior: participate in therapy, join a self-help group; take medication; remove myself from

situations of temptation; change jobs;
change my lifestyle.

Accept forgiveness: Receive forgiveness as a gift
and rejoice in it; be healed; embrace wholeness; bear witness to God's love.

Discuss the value and importance of each stage, sug-
gesting ways people might do them.

Endnotes

∼ **Chapter 2: How to Use the Series**

1. Discipleship Groups was developed by national church staff in partnership with the Dioceses of California and Delaware. It is a resource that can help your congregation start a small group ministry, and is available through LeaderResources (800-941-2218). It includes a twelve-session training program for small group leaders and twelve introductory sessions. The first six sessions focus on the baptismal covenant; the second six sessions focus on ministry in daily life. These sessions encourage the kind of personal sharing and prayer together that foster bonding in small groups. Once the group has reached the thirteenth session, it chooses one of The New Church's Teaching Series books as the focus for its next set of six to eight sessions.

2. EFM is a four-year program of theological education offered by the School of Theology at the University of the South in Sewanee, Tennessee (800-722-1974).

3. For the liturgical rites and an explanation of each stage of the catechumenal process, see *The Book of*

Occasional Services (New York: Church Publishing, 1994), 144ff.

4. The *Episcopal Youth Curriculum* is available from Morehouse Publishing Group (800-877-0012).

5. *Journey to Adulthood* is available from Leader-Resources (800-941-2218).

6. This program for lay eucharistic ministers is available from LeaderResources (800-941-2218).

7. For Daughters of the King, contact 770-419-8580. For information about the Order of St. Luke, call 210-492-5222.

8. Faith Comes By Hearing has a program in which you can purchase the entire Bible on tapes or CD. In addition to listening to them, you can use them as a fundraiser by signing up pledges for each hour of listening. The funds raised can then be used locally or given to Faith Comes By Hearing to produce tapes in languages where most of the population does not read and thus does not have access to the Bible. For more information call 800-545-6552.

～ **Chapter 3: Establishing and Leading Groups**

1. The Center for the Ministry of Teaching at Virginia Seminary may be reached at 703-461-1750. The Episcopal Media Center may be reached at 404-633-7800.

2. The following discussion on asking questions is adapted from Linda L. Grenz, *Mentoring the Marriage Journey* (Leeds, Mass.: LeaderResources, 1996).

～ **Chapter 4: Various Formats for Using the Books**

1. *In Dialogue With Scripture* is published by the Episcopal Church and is available from Episcopal Parish Services (800-903-5544). *The Doubleday Pocket Bible Guide* by Linda L. Grenz is available from

LeaderResources (800-941-2218) or your local bookstore. Each of these has more than a dozen different
Bible study methods that can be self-led or facilitated
by small group leaders.

2. *Better Safe Than Sued* by Jack Crabtree is available
from its publisher, Group Publishing, or from
LeaderResources, 800-941-2218.

∾ **Chapter 5: Suggested Activities for
Each Volume**

1. The Episcopal Media Center (404-633-7800) has
several recordings of the gospel of Mark, and you can
obtain the entire New Testament on audiotape or CD-
ROM from Faith Comes By Hearing (800-545-6552).
You may also be able to borrow a Mark video from the
Center for the Ministry of Teaching at Virginia
Seminary (703-461-1750).

2. *In Dialogue With Scripture* is available from
Episcopal Parish Services (800-903-5544). It also
includes an extensive list of Bible resources that your
group may want to use as a follow-up to reading this
book. *The Doubleday Pocket Bible Guide* is available
from your local bookstore; it also includes a short
summary of and key verses in each book of the Bible.

3. The National Association of Biblical Storytellers can
be contacted at: NOBS, 1810 Harvard Blvd., Dayton,
Ohio 45406; 800-355-NOBS or 937-278-5127; Fax:
937- 278-1218; e-mail: nobsint@nobs.org; webpage:
www.nobs.org.

4. The following is adapted from *The Journey to
Adulthood* youth program, Rite-13 Lessons 8 and 9 on
Compassion and Acts of Mercy.

5. We often call countries in the southern hemisphere
"third-world countries" but this implies a hierarchy
and status difference that can be avoided by using the
neutral term "southern" instead.

6. Robert McAfee Brown, *Unexpected News: Reading the Bible with Third World Eyes* (Philadelphia: Westminster, 1988).

Cowley Publications is a ministry of the Society of St. John the Evangelist, a religious community for men in the Episcopal Church. Emerging from the Society's tradition of prayer, theological reflection, and diversity of mission, the press is centered in the rich heritage of the Anglican Communion.

Cowley Publications seeks to provide books, audio cassettes, and other resources for the ongoing theological exploration and spiritual development of the Episcopal Church and others in the body of Christ. To this end, it is dedicated to developing a new generation of theological writers, encouraging them to produce timely, creative, and stimulating publications of excellence, and making these publications available widely, reaching both clergy and lay persons.